TSUYOSHI TANE

Archaeology
of the
Future

TOTO出版

TSUYOSHI TANE   Archaeology of the Future

First edition published in Japan on October 24, 2018
First edition, fifth printing published on February 17, 2025

Author: Tsuyoshi Tane

Publisher: Akira Watai
TOTO Publishing (TOTO LTD.)
TOTO Nogizaka Bldg., 2F
1-24-3 Minami-Aoyama, Minato-ku Tokyo 107-0062, Japan
[Sales] Telephone: +81-3-3402-7138 Facsimile: +81-3-3402-7187
[Editorial] Telephone: +81-3-3497-1010
URL: https://jp.toto.com/publishing

Designer: Takuma Hayashi
Printer: Sannichi Printing Co., Ltd.

Except as permitted under copyright law, this book may not be
reproduced, in whole or in part, in any form or by any means,
including photocopying, scanning, digitizing, or otherwise, without
prior permission. Scanning or digitizing this book through a third
party, even for personal or home use, is also strictly prohibited. The
list price is indicated on the cover.

ISBN978-4-88706-376-1

Archaeology of the Future
未来の記憶

We aspire to create architecture nobody has ever seen, experienced, or even imagined yet. However, it is not novel and futuristic architecture we are after. We are taking a broader perspective to materialize architecture originating in memories of a place.

As a first step, we travel back in time and excavate the past to find memories embedded in a place like archaeologists. It is a surprizing and joyful process of searching to encounter and deeply getting to know what we didn't know, what we had forgotten, and what we had lost due to modernization and globalization. There are always memories in the place that deeply embedded beneath the ground. Then that archaeology, the process of thinking in depth from the past to the future, slowly becomes architecture.

Now, we began to be convinced that memories are not things to belong in the past, but it is a driving force to create architecture of the future. It is architecture in memories of a place — we call it "Archaeology of the Future."

まだ誰も見たことのない、経験したこともない、想像すらしたことのない、そんな建築をつくりたいと思っています。でもそれは新しい未来型の建築とは違う、場所の記憶からつくる未来の建築、そんな途方もないことを考えています。

そのために私は、考古学者のように時間を過去に向かって遡り、場所の記憶を掘り起こすことから始めます。それは発見のプロセスであり、そこには自分たちが知らないもの、忘れ去ってしまったもの、または近代化やグローバル化によって今日の世界から消えてしまったものに遭遇し、驚き、それらを発掘する喜びがあるのです。場所には必ず記憶があり、深い思考と考察から記憶を未来へ向けることによって、記憶はゆっくりと建築になっていくのです。

記憶は過去のものではなく、未来をつくる原動力だと思い始めました。
私は場所の記憶から考える未来の建築を「Archaeology of the Future」と呼んでいます。

Contents

Manifesto 006

Concepts 015

Images 113

Drawings 263

Timeline 307

Credits 317

Acknowledgement

Profile

Architecture is Place

When architecture is born, a place is born.

A long time ago, humans erected a stone on the earth, inserted a log into the field and dug a hole in the ground. This was the beginning of architecture. Through these inventions, humans created places called "here."
When people started gathering in the places called "here", society began, cities were founded, and civilizations developed.

Humans began to understand that by building architecture, a meaning is given to a place, and then that place has a story that can be passed on to others.

Architecture creates a place, and a place accepts all events.

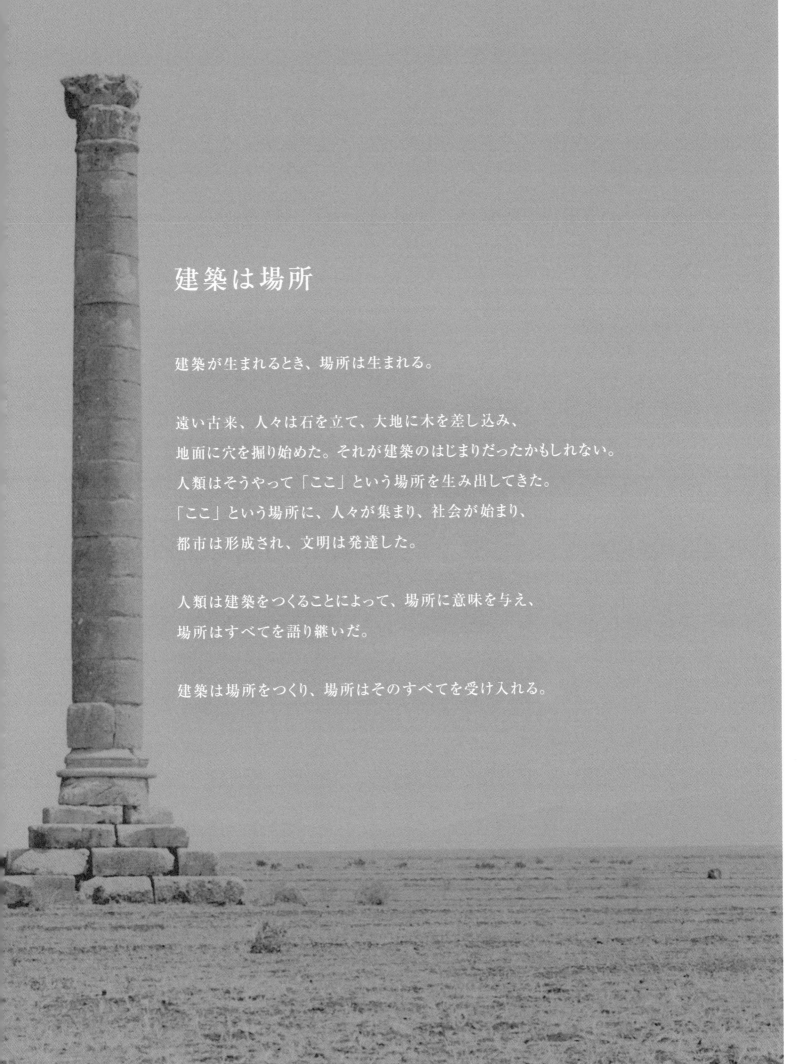

建築は場所

建築が生まれるとき、場所は生まれる。

遠い古来、人々は石を立て、大地に木を差し込み、
地面に穴を掘り始めた。それが建築のはじまりだったかもしれない。
人類はそうやって「ここ」という場所を生み出してきた。
「ここ」という場所に、人々が集まり、社会が始まり、
都市は形成され、文明は発達した。

人類は建築をつくることによって、場所に意味を与え、
場所はすべてを語り継いだ。

建築は場所をつくり、場所はそのすべてを受け入れる。

Architecture is Future

Architecture creates the future.

When architecture is born, the future of a place begins.
The future of a place instigates renewal of architecture.
Architecture, in a constant search of newness, drove new eras forward, became a source of desires, and formed new civilizations where new architectures were continuously created.

In the Ancient times, as a symbol of power.
In the Medieval times, as an enlightenment of religion.
In Industrial times, as an invention of technology.
In Modern times, as an investment of capitalization.
And today, as an accumulation of information.

Architecture creates a new era, and a new era anticipates the future by creating architecture.

建築は未来

建築は未来をつくる。

建築が生まれることで場所の未来が始まる。
場所の未来は、建築を新しくさせてきた。
建築は新しさを求め、時代の動力となり、欲望となって
新しい文明が新しい建築をつくり続けた。

古代は権力の象徴として
中世は宗教の啓蒙として
近世は産業の開拓として
近代は資本の投下として
現代は情報の集積として

建築が時代をつくり、時代は建築によって未来を予感させる。

Architecture is Memory

Architecture, when it is created, gives memories to a place.

All civilizations, eras and societies have continuously built architecture. Architecture has been passed down from generation to generation, forming the genes of our society from collective memories that convey the traces of time.

But today, too many things have been modernized and too much has been lost in our society and culture. With a massive overflow of information, continued land exploitation and climate changes, we can no longer trust the future through only modernity.
When architecture is lost, its future and memories are lost and its place will be forgotten. We may have forgotten many things and architecture must exist to perpetuate and sustain the collective memories of time and place.

Even if we have lost everything, only memories can give us a way to start the future.

建築は記憶

建築が生まれることで、建築は場所に記憶を与える。

どの文明も、どの時代も、どの社会も建築を常につくり続けた。
建築は時代を超え、人から人へ、世代から世代へと受け継がれ、
時間の記憶装置として社会や文化の遺伝子となり続けてきた。

しかし、いまわれわれは多くのものを新しくし、多くのものを失い過ぎた。
膨大な情報が溢れ、土地の開発を繰り返し、地球環境が変動するなかで、
新しいだけでは、未来を信じることができなくなった。
建築を失うと、未来を失い、記憶を失い、そしていつか場所を忘れる。
人類は物事を忘れてきたが、建築は時間を場所に記憶してきた。

すべてを失い、何もない場所に立ち尽くしたとき、
記憶だけがわれわれに未来を与える。

Architecture is Archaeology of the Future

Architecture holds memories of the future.

Memories of the future in architecture inspire us to envision the further future. Architecture began from memories of the place, and architecture transforms into memories of the future.

To create the architecture of a more meaningful further future, perhaps we must; excavate the memories of a place, rather than thoughtless renewal, transform memories into the future, rather than keeping memories in the past, and dive in to the past to think of the future, rather than only looking forward. At that moment, memories are no longer a thing of the past, but gradually become a driving force to the future.

Architecture perpetuates memories of a place, and architecture becomes archaeology of the future.

建築は未来の記憶

建築は未来を記憶する。

建築の記憶は未来のその先にある未来を想起させる。
建築は場所の記憶から始まり、建築は未来の記憶へと変貌する。

場所を無碍に更地にするより、場所の記憶を発掘する着想が、
記憶を過去に留めるより、記憶を未来へと飛躍させる想像力が、
未来を新しさから創造するより、未来を古来から発想する信念が、
建築をより深く、より長く、より遠い未来へと導き始める。
その時、記憶は過去のものではなく、記憶は未来への力となる。

建築は場所を記憶し、建築は未来の記憶となる。

Concepts

Estonian National Museum
エストニア国立博物館
16

Kofun Stadium - New National Stadium Japan
新国立競技場案　古墳スタジアム
24

10 kyoto
10 kyoto
30

Wonderground -
Natural History Museum of Denmark
Wonderground - デンマーク自然科学博物館
36

Arthur Rimbaud Museum
アルチュール・ランボー美術館
42

Hirosaki Contemporary Art Museum
（仮称）弘前市芸術文化施設
48

Shibuya Department Store
渋谷デパートメントストア
54

Twin Towers in Kai Tak Development
カイタック・ツインタワー
60

Yokohama Station Department Store
（仮称）横浜駅デパートメントストア
66

Chiso Building
千總本社ビル
72

A House for Oiso
A House for Oiso
78

Todoroki House in Valley
Todoroki House in Valley
84

Weekend House in Fontainebleau
フォンテーヌブロー週末住宅
90

Toraya Paris
とらやパリ店
96

Luce Tempo Luogo
Luce Tempo Luogo
100

LIGHT is TIME
LIGHT is TIME
104

time is TIME
time is TIME
108

Estonian National Museum

エストニア国立博物館 | Tartu, Estonia 2006-16 | museum completed

After Estonia declared independence in 1991, they made a promise to build a new national museum as a symbol of the nation and a place to preserve the people's memories. While most countries in the world choose to renovate historic buildings into national museums, Estonia made a bold decision to build a new national museum and held an international design competition. The designated site was located at Raadi district in the northeast part of the city of Tartu, where the remains of the first national museum, a converted former manor house of a noble German Family, had existed from 1920-1940. After 1940 a Soviet military base occupied approximately 692 hectares of the site and the museum building was destroyed and the collection hidden throughout the country. The airfield's long runway was laid out in the middle of the desolate ground that cut through the forests. Instead of eliminating or being oblivious to this negative heritage, we connected the new Estonian National Museum to the edge of the runway to extend it, in order to pass the Estonian people's memories to the future. The ground slowly rises and takes off from the Soviet era military runway, symbolizing the history, and extends into the sky to create architecture for the future. This project was named "Memory Field," and plays a role in handing down people's memories through generations, gives new meaning to the place that was once occupied land, and connects the collective memories to the future.
Our proposal "Memory Field" was chosen as the winner of the international design competition in 2006 and opened ten years later, on October 1, 2016.

エストニアは1991年の独立後、国立博物館の建設を国民に約束した。国の象徴であると同時に長きにわたる民族の記憶となる国立博物館の建物には、世界のほとんどの国が歴史的建造物を転用しているのに対し、エストニアは大胆にも国際設計競技による国立博物館の新築に挑んだ。敷地には、1909年に旧ドイツ領主の館を転用した最初の国立博物館の痕跡が残るタルトゥ市の北東のラディ地区が選ばれた。そこはかつてソビエト連邦の軍用地として約692haにわたり占拠され、荒涼とした大地の中央には滑走路が森を切り裂くように横たわっていた。その負の遺産である旧ソ連の軍用滑走路を抹消するわけでもなく、忘却するでもなく、エストニアの民族の記憶を継承するように博物館を滑走路の延長線として接続した。軍用滑走路という受難の歴史から、ゆっくりと大地が隆起し、空へ向かって延びていく未来の建築となる。このプロジェクトは「メモリーフィールド（記憶の原野）」と名付けられ、民族の記憶が世代から世代へと受け継がれ、負の遺産である場所の意味を転化し、エストニアの未来への記憶をつなぐ建築となる。
2006年1月16日、この「メモリーフィールド」は国際設計競技にて最優秀案として選ばれ、約10年の歳月を掛け2016年10月1日に開館した。

The first Estonian National Museum established in 1909 in Tartu, Estonia　エストニア、タルトゥに1909年に設立された最初のエストニア国立博物館

Tartu House　タルトゥの住居

Detail of Tartu House　タルトゥの住居詳細

Traditional Seto Singers　伝統的なセトの歌い手

Officials of ENM in national costume　伝統衣装姿のスタッフ (1941)

Field survey　現地調査の様子 (1913)

Collection of traditional tankards　伝統工芸ジョッキのコレクション (1923)

Early Photo Exhibition at ENM　エストニア国立博物館での写真展 (1913)

Daily's tools on display　生活用具の展示風景 (1923)

Sketch of the traditional pattern of the Mulgi region　ムルギ地方で用いられてる伝統柄のスケッチ

Memories of Estonians that have been preserved in deep forests in the form of wood, textile and song.
北の深い森の中で継承されてきたエストニアの民族の記憶。木を刻み、布に色を与え、鉄を叩き、魂を歌にしてきた民族の物語。

The Stone Bridge in Tartu city　タルトゥ市内のストーンブリッジ

Former USSR Raadi Military field　旧ソ連ラディ地区軍用地

Raadi Military Airfield　ラディ地区軍用滑走路

Aerial view of Raadi Military Airfield　ラディ地区軍用滑走路空撮

Protest at Raadi Base　ラディ基地での抗議運動

Townspeople heading to march　デモ行進をする地区住民

"Free Raadi, 1 May"　10日間にわたる「フリーラディ運動」(1989)

"The Baltic Way"　バルト三国独立運動「バルトの道」(1989.08.23)

Occupation is the deprivation of a place. Even when people are deprived of a place, their memories cannot be erased.
占領とは圧力による場所の略奪である。人は場所の上で生きている。場所は奪われても、人びとの記憶を消すことはできない。

Concept sketch　コンセプトスケッチ

When architecture is born, the future is born. Architecture creates the future.
ひとつの建築が生まれる。建築が生まれるとき未来が生まれる。未来は建築によって生まれ、建築は未来をつくることができる。

負の歴史を忘却するでもなく、抹消するでもなく、未来につなげる。歴史は過去に残るが、場所の記憶は未来をつくる原動力である。

Site photo　敷地写真

The negative past is not buried but connected to the future. History stays in the past but memories of a place create the future.
負の歴史を忘却するでもなく、抹消するでもなく、未来につなげる。歴史は過去に残るが、場所の記憶は未来をつくる原動力である。

Concept model　コンセプト模型

A new architecture is born on the desolate military base. It slowly rises from the runway and takes off into the sky towards the future.
荒涼とした軍用地に新しい建築が生まれる。滑走路から未来へと飛び立つような、大地から空へと消えていくような建築。

Model　模型

Plenty of public spaces are provided that go beyond typical functions promoting ENM's role as a national museum for the 21st century.
建築の内部に無数のパブリックスペースをつくる。民族品の収集・展示・保存を超えた21世紀のナショナルミュージアムを目指している。

Kofun Stadium - New National Stadium Japan

新国立競技場案　古墳スタジアム　|　Tokyo, Japan　2012　|　stadium　international competition, finalist

The origin of stadiums goes back to Ancient Greece, where people excavated the ground to build places to gather. Stadiums were built as a part of urban development in Greek cities and were intended to serve as a festival venue and a place for citizens to celebrate special events. In 2012 the Japanese government decided to demolish its former National Stadium, the main venue for the 1964 Tokyo Olympics & Paralympics. The site would be used for a New National Stadium to serve as the main venue for the 2020 Tokyo Olympics & Paralympics. Their goal was to recreate an "architecture for people to gather at the center of the city". The site is situated within Meiji Jingu Gaien, the outer precinct of the Meiji Shrine. While Meiji Jingu Naien, or the inner precinct, was developed as a sacred grove of the Meiji Shrine, Jingu Gaien was developed as a place to promote cultural/sports activities and to create the future of Tokyo. However, over the years the original significance of Jingu Gaien has been gradually forgotten. We proposed "Kofun Stadium", inspired by *kofun* or the ancient burial mounds in Japan, with the aim of regaining the significance of this place. Kofun Stadium integrates the Olympics, the largest sports festival in the world, and *kofun*, the largest ancient construction in Japan, equivalent to the scale of the pyramids of Giza. This architecture is a grand vision of delivering the memory of this place to Tokyo. It helps to create the city's future by introducing a forest that will develop for 100 years: trees would be collected from all over Japan to be planted by citizens' hands, following the development method of the Meiji Jingu forest.

2012年夏、東京2020オリンピック・パラリンピック招致に向けて、「新国立競技場基本構想国際デザイン競技」が行われた。競技場の起源は古代ギリシアに始まり、大地を削り、人びとが集まる場所をつくった。競技場は祭典の場として、市民の非日常の場所として、ギリシア都市形成の一部として生み出された。2020年東京オリンピックでは、1964年の東京オリンピックの時に建てられたメイン会場の国立競技場を解体し建て替えることで、再び都心部に人が集まる場所の次世代型の競技場を目指していた。この地域は明治神宮外苑の敷地内でもあり、明治神宮は内苑に明治天皇の鎮魂の場として人工の杜を造り、神宮外苑は文化とスポーツ振興の場として東京の未来へと開かれていた。さまざまな時代の変遷により、その場所の意味を失いかけていた神宮外苑に21世紀の新国立競技場として「古墳スタジアム」を提案した。古墳は中国文明が渡来する以前の日本の古代社会がつくった最大の建造物である。そこで現在世界で最大の祭典となるオリンピックと古代最大の日本のピラミッドである古墳が一体となる建築を提案した。その建築は、明治神宮の森のつくり方に倣い、日本の各地から木々を集め、民の手によって100年の森をつくるナショナル・プロジェクトとすることで場所の記憶を未来へ向ける夢の構想であった。

Bunkyu Sanryo zu by Tsurusawa Tanshin, which is the drawing of the tombs that exist in various parts of Japan　全国各地の墳墓を描いた『文久山陵図』鶴澤探眞

Stadium reclamation work　競技場敷地工事の様子 (1920's)

Site Maintenance　敷地整備状況 (1920's)

Large black pine transplant work　大黒松移植作業 (1920's)

View from Aoyama Entrance　青山口からの景色 (1920's)

Youth groups gathered from various places　各地から集められた青年団による作業風景 (1920's)

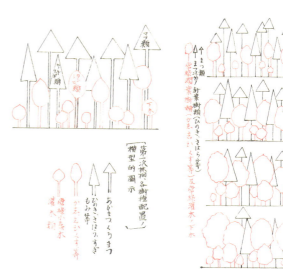
Woods garden plan inside Meiji Jingu　明治神宮御境内林苑計画

Meiji Jingu Gaien plan　明治神宮外苑平面図

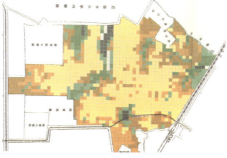
Soil survey in Meiji Jingu Gaien　明治神宮外苑敷地土性調査図

Meiji Jingu Gaien Stadium　明治神宮外苑競技場 (1924)

The Meiji Jingu Forest was born on vacant land. A place starts from an idea, and an idea transforms the future into the present.
神宮の森は何もないところから始まった。ある場所が生まれるとき、すべては構想から始まる。構想は時代を超えて未来を現実にする。

Daisen Kofun, the Tomb of Emperor Nintoku, constructed around 5C, Osaka　5世紀頃につくられた仁徳天皇陵「大仙陵古墳」、大阪

Did ancient people imagine future humans would see kofun? Did they know memories of the future are made by architecture?
古代の人びとは未来の人類が古墳をみることを想像していたのだろうか。建築をつくることが未来の記憶をつくることを古代人は知っていたのだろうか。

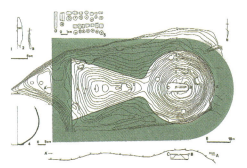
Kofun analysis drawing　古墳の分析図

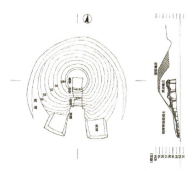
Obusan Kofun reconstruction drawing　オブサン古墳墳丘復原図

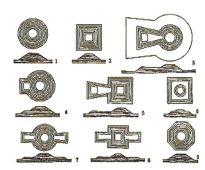
Forms of kofun　古墳の形態図

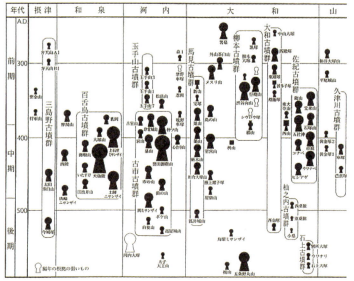
Chronology of large kofuns in Kinai area　畿内における大型古墳の編年

Stone artifacts from Ishiyama Kofun, Mie　石山古墳出土石製品と石製模造品、三重

Athens Olympic Stadium　アテネオリンピックスタジアム

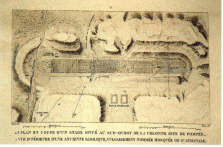
Hippodrome of Alexandria　アレクサンドリアのヒッポロドーム

Pianta del Circo Massimo　ピアンタ・サーカス劇場

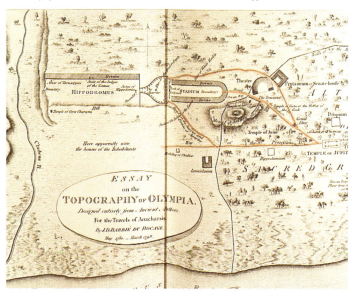
Drawing showing topography of ancient Olympia　古代オリンピックの地形図

Opening ceremony of Athens Olympics　アテネオリンピックの開会式

Architecture can connect with the ground by raising or digging. Unrelated typologies, a stadium and kofun become one architecture.
地形を盛ることと地形を掘ることで建築は大地とつながる。古代日本の古墳と古代ギリシアの競技場という無関係なものが建築によってひとつになる。

A large mound unexpectedly appears in the center of Tokyo. We envisioned that the future of Tokyo would start from here.
東京の中心に山ができる。それは突然でもあり、そこから東京の未来が始まると考えていた。

Model of New National Stadium in Tokyo　新国立競技場案模型、東京

10 kyoto

10 kyoto | Kyoto, Japan 2017- | complex ongoing

We are planning a building in the form of a cross-shaped pyramid in Jujo, Kyoto. Kyoto is a city with a 1200 year-history based on a street grid system of major and minor streets. From Ancient Mesopotamia to Modernist urban planning, the urban grid system had been incorporated in city centers as a basic infrastructure of civilization. We started this project by re-examining the historical transition of the city of Kyoto from "Heian-kyo" (the official capital city of Japan from 794 to 1868) to the present city with a focus on "jo" (streets running east-west) or the horizontal urban axis. Urban layers of Kyoto divided along "jo" or the east-west axis from Ichijo (the first avenue) to Kujo (the ninth avenue) reveal different phases of Kyoto's development through history and how memories of the places have changed over time. Jujo (the tenth avenue) was given its official name in 1912, but this new part of Kyoto had been unknown to most people for over a hundred years. The surrounding area is a wide gray-colored expanse of industrial zones, totally detached from Kyoto's history and tradition as well as urban development. It is within this environment that we are building a new architecture integrating art, food, and a lifestyle with the aim of promoting contemporary culture in Kyoto. We are studying the possibilities of a cross-shaped pyramid form, originating in ancient architecture, as a potential for creating the future of Kyoto. This facility is being developed as a cultural factory where old neglected items in Kyoto will be collected and reused to create Kyoto's culture for the new era.

京都十条に十字のピラミッド型の建築を計画している。1200年の歴史をもつ京都は、大路小路による条坊制でつくられたグリッドシティである。グリッドシステムによる都市計画は場所性にとらわれない厳格なシステムであり、古代メソポタミアに始まり近代都市計画までさまざまな文明の基盤装置としてグリッドシステムは都市の中心に組み込まれてきた。平安京から時代とともに変遷してきた京都を「条」による横軸の歴史で読みかえる試みから始めた。一条から九条まで東西軸の「条」で分割していく京都は、さまざまな時代の揺らぎと記憶の変貌を物語る。一方で十条は1912年に京都の南に新しく命名されたが知られざる京都として100年以上の時間が過ぎ去った。周辺地域は京都の歴史や伝統から切り離され、開発からも取り残され、工場地帯が広がっている。ここに古い京都を集め、新しい京都の現代文化を発するような建築をつくろうとしている。京都で解体された建物の大量の古材を集め集成材とする「古材集成材」が建物全体を覆い、古き財産を集め新しい文化に変えるプロジェクトを計画している。

Tikal, Province of Petén, Guatemala　マヤ文明の中心都市ティカル、グアテマラ

Map of Gion Shrine　祇園神社境内絵図

Rakuchurakugaizu by Kano Eitoku　「洛中洛外図」狩野永徳 (1565)

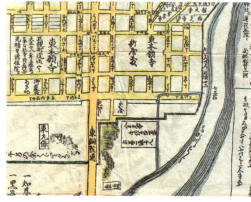
Map of Jujo area in Kyoto　京都十条地区 (1696)

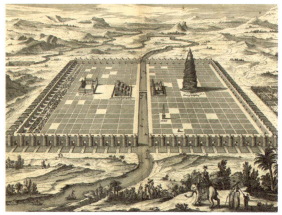
Aerial view of Babylon　古代都市バビロンの俯瞰図

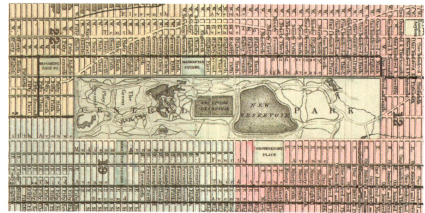
Map of New York　ニューヨークの地図 (1882)

Chichen Itza Pyramid　マヤ文明のピラミッド

Ancient coins　古代の貨幣

Cross shaped applique　十字型アップリケ (600)

Laminated reclaimed wood　古材集成材

Stairway of intellect　知性の階段 (1304)

Pyramid on the Saone　ソーヌ川上のピラミッド (16C)

Ventilation system of mines　鉱山の空調システム図

As an urban system, the grid city originated in Mesopotamian embedded intelligence, reason, desire and oblivion of future cities.
メソポタミア文明より始まったグリッドシティは都市管理システムとして人類の知性と理性と欲望、そして忘却を都市の未来に組み込んだ。

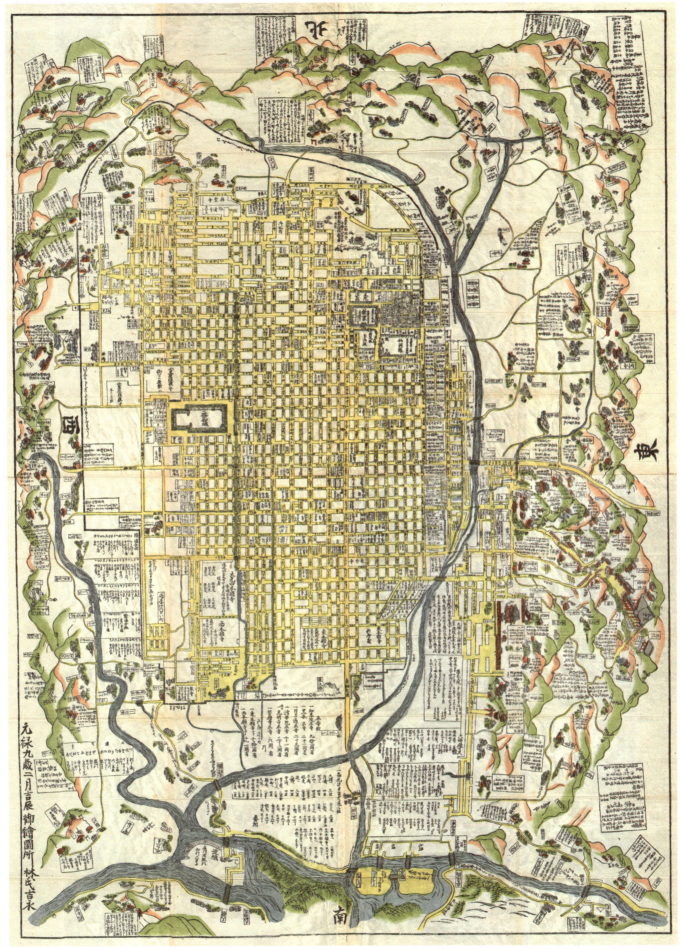

Map of Kyoto 京都の地図 (1696)

Kyoto is a 1200-year old grid city. There are deep memories in the layers of the past that give dignity to the city.
京都は1200年前から続くグリッドシティである。歴史の重なりが都市の記憶を深め、記憶が都市に尊厳を与えてきた。

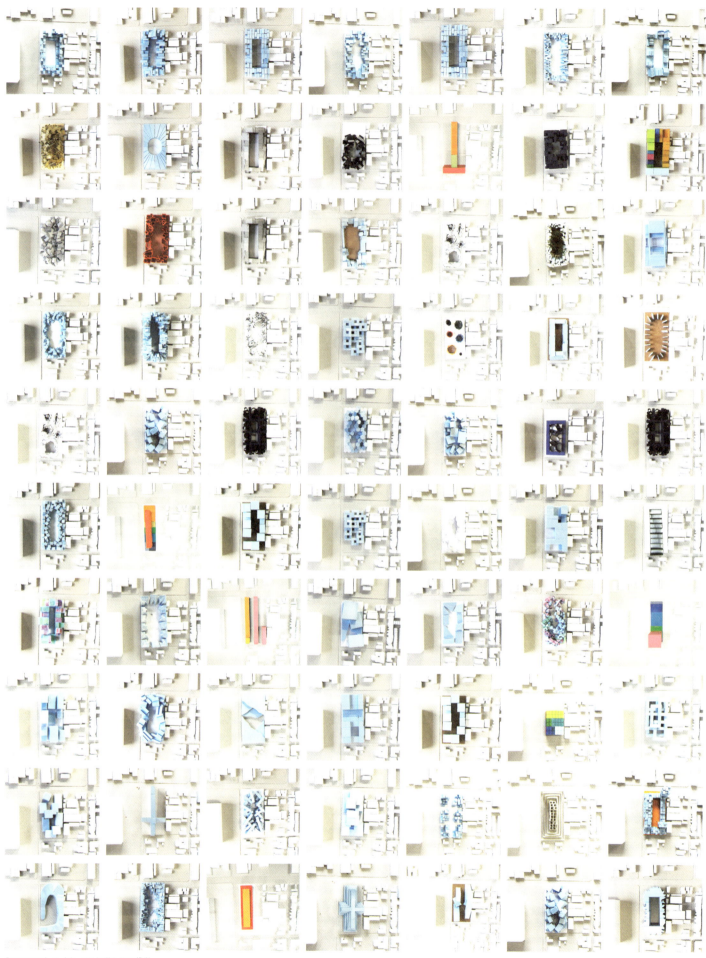

Concept study models　コンセプトスタディ模型

We began by making a cluster of kyo-machiya but somehow orientated towards an unknown kind of architecture through model studies.
京町家の集合体をつくるところから始めた。町家の集積を目指したはずが、段々と模型をつくるうちに、未知なる建築へと向かっていった。

"十"のピラミッドが出来上がる。古代の形式で未来の建築をつくろうとしている。最も古い力こそが永遠なる未来なのかもしれない。

Concept model　コンセプト模型

"+" shaped pyramid - a future architecture can be created by an ancient one. The oldest form may show us the further future.
「十」のピラミッドが出来上がる。古代の形式で未来の建築をつくろうとしている。最も古い力こそが永遠なる未来なのかもしれない。

Wonderground - Natural History Museum of Denmark

Wonderground - デンマーク自然科学博物館 | Copenhagen, Denmark 2009 | museum international competition

"It is not the strongest of the species that survives, not the most intelligent that survives. It is the one that is the most adaptable to change." — Charles Darwin. The history of man's habit of collecting things in the field of natural science goes back to the 16th century, when they started excavating the ground and collecting findings out of curiosity. Soon after, people began analyzing nature based on a scientific method and started taxonomy in order to systematically categorize differences. Evolution is a result of sequential differentiations. The study of natural history began when they started archiving observational records of various things including micro-bacteria, macro astronomical bodies, dinosaur fossils, and fragments of meteorites. The Natural Museum of Denmark is situated on a place where many remains of fortresses and historic landmarks built between the 12th century to the 17th century when the city of Copenhagen prospered due to foreign trades and the power of Kingdom, are preserved. For this reason, the design requirement given by the international design competition was contradictory; we were requested to plan a new museum without constructing buildings. Our design started from creating spaces by digging into the ground, without constructing new spaces. The museum was designed in such a way that visitors can feel the excitement of simultaneously experiencing wonders of natural science and architecture by providing a series of exhibition spaces where its scales are proportional to the sizes of the exhibits under different themes.

最も強い者が生き残るのではなく、最も賢い者が生き延びるのでもない。唯一生き残ることができるのは、変化できる者である。──チャールズ・ダーウィン

人類の自然科学の収集癖の歴史は、好奇心による発掘と発見によって「収集」を起源として16世紀より始まる。その一方で、科学は自然を分析することによって、万物の差異を系統化する分類学を始めた。進化は分化の連続として、ミクロなバクテリアからマクロな天体、恐竜の化石から隕石までの数々の物質の観測記録を保存することによって博物史が生まれる。デンマーク自然科学博物館は、コペンハーゲンの都市が12世紀から17世紀にかけて王国の交易港として築かれた要塞の痕跡と歴史的建造物が多く残る場所にあり、建物をつくらずに新たな博物館の計画が要望される矛盾した内容の国際コンペであった。そこで建築全体を発掘現場のように、地面を掘り込むことで空間を構築せずに、空間を発掘するような建築から考え始めた。空間は自然科学のミクロからマクロまでの物質の大小がそのまま空間のスケールとして連動することで、自然科学の驚きと建築が一体となる試みを提案した。

Sir Ashton Lever's Museum, London　アシュトン・レバー卿の博物館、ロンドン (1785)

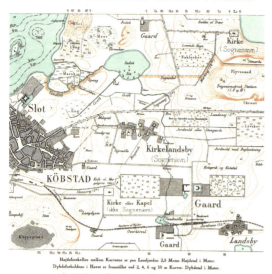
Survey map of Copenhagen　コペンハーゲンの測量地図 (1940)

Map of Copenhagen　コペンハーゲンの地図 (1728)

Copenhagen Botanical Garden　コペンハーゲン植物園平面図

Museum Wormiani Historia　オーレ・ワームの歴史博物館 (1655)

Natural history museum in Naples　ナポリ自然史博物館 (1672)

Milkwort and sea heath　ヒメハギとヒース (1855)

Illustration of ancient creatures　古代生物のイラスト (1830)

Plant Room of the British Museum　大英博物館植物室 (1858)

Bullock's Museum　ブロックス博物館 (1810)

Fossil mining in England　イングランドでの化石採掘 (1784)

Evolution is differentiation. Natural history defined evolution by collecting, classifying and studying differences.
進化は分化から始まる。自然科学は、多種多様な自然物の全てを掻き集め、分類し、差異を研究することで進化の過程を探り続けてきた。

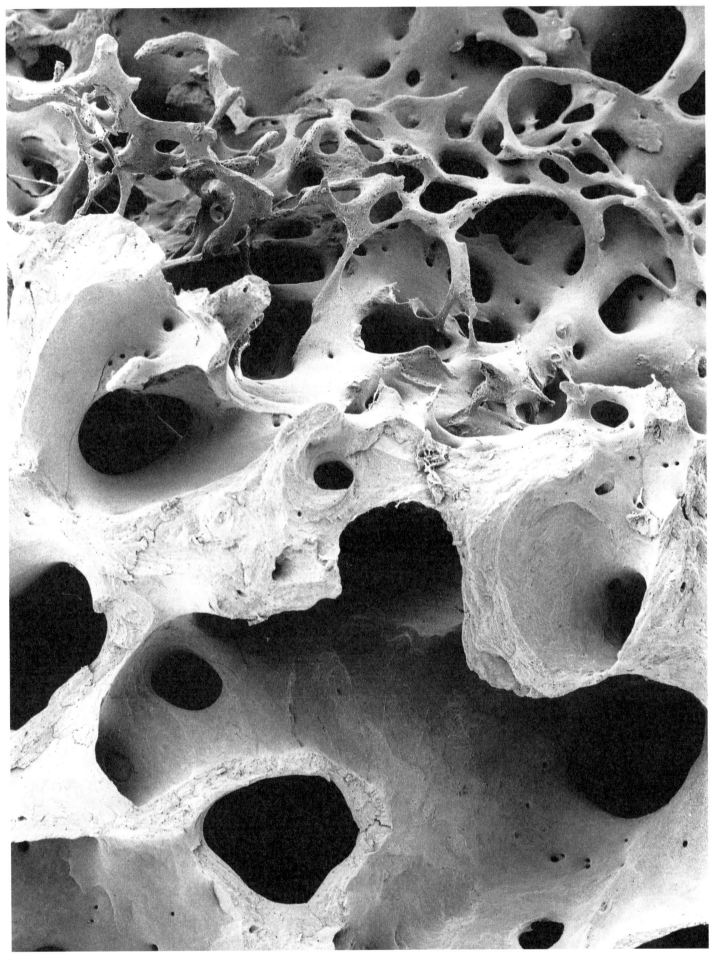

SEM of cancellous bone tissue　電子顕微鏡でみた海綿骨組織

Topography is created by erosion and plate tectonics. Architecture can be created not only by construction but also by excavation.
地形は変動と侵食によって生まれる。建築は「Construction（建てる）」だけではなく、「Excavation（掘る）」によってつくることも可能である。

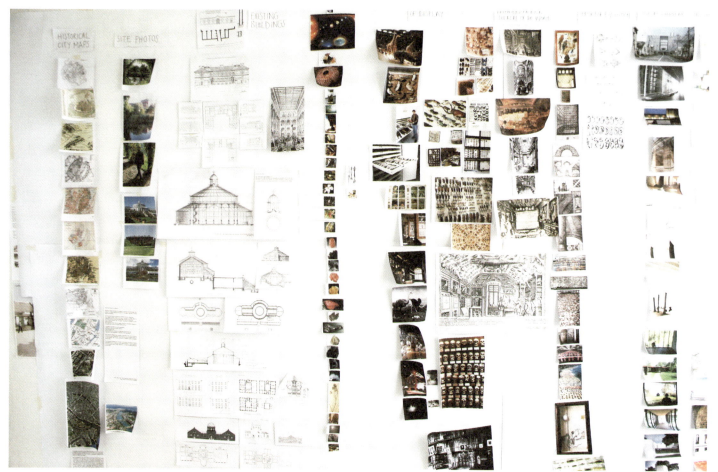

Archaeological Research-Classification　アーキオロジカルリサーチ ─ 分類

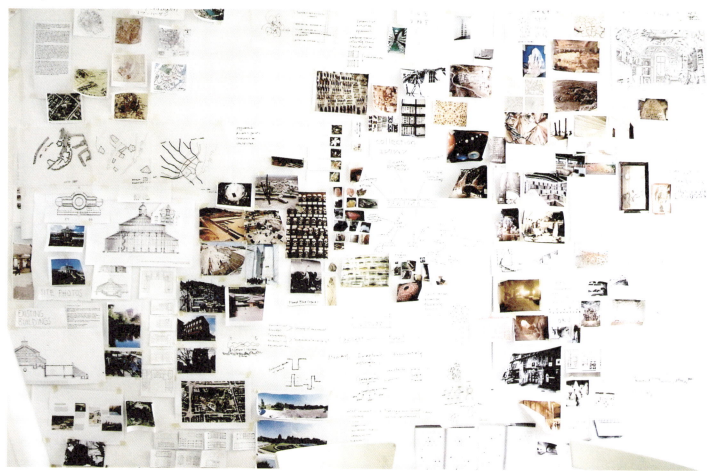

Archaeological Research-Evolution　アーキオロジカルリサーチ ─ 発展

We came up with "Archaeological Research" in 2009. It is an archaeological method applied to the process of architecture research.
2009年、この時初めて「Archaeological Research」のアイデアが生まれた。これは未来を考古学的にリサーチする発掘作業である。

空間を構築することと空間を発掘することは同じかもしれない。ArchaeologyとArchitectureがひとつにつながっていく。

Concept model　コンセプト模型

Construction and excavation of spaces may be the same thing. Archaeology and architecture are gradually integrated.
空間を構築することと空間を発掘することは同じかもしれない。ArchaeologyとArchitectureがひとつにつながっていく。

Arthur Rimbaud Museum

アルチュール・ランボー美術館 | Charleville-Mézières, France 2012 | museum competition, 2nd prize

This project for the museum of the 19th century French poet Arthur Rimbaud was a plan to convert a watermill, a historic landmark in his hometown of Charleville-Mézières, into a museum of poetry. Rimbaud left this town at a young age, went adrift and sacrificed his stable life to keep writing poems. His poetry, with characteristic aggressive expressions that stir up and tear apart one's feelings and the brilliant use of words, has had significant influence across generations from his contemporaries to our contemporaries. Rimbaud, who had spent most of his life on the road, left few personal effects except his poetry. The dramatic quality of Rimbaud's poetry and life is further intensified by the absence of physical objects as visitors look back at the trajectory of his life course in this museum. Our design of the watermill introduced the concept of renovating the interior of the historic landmark by "destruction." All spaces are centered around the large atrium space serving as a "theater." A lack of materiality in the world of poetry is converted into and communicated through theatrical expressions such as performances and poetry readings. Rimbaud once said "I is another." In this museum, all visitors are spectators and actors at the same time.

19世紀のフランスの詩人、アルチュール・ランボーの美術館は、彼の生まれ故郷であるシャルルヴィル・メツィエの記念碑的な水車小屋を改修して計画される「詩」の美術館であった。ランボーは若くしてこの街を去り、生活を犠牲にし、路頭に迷いながら、詩を書き続け、言葉が感情を揺るがし切り裂くような詩の過激性と言葉の輝きによって同時代から現代に至るまで多くの影響を与えることとなった。人生の大半を旅路で過ごしたランボーの数少ない遺品が「詩」であるという物質の不在、そしてランボーの人生を追憶する体験が、ランボーの劇性を高める美術館であり劇場空間となる。彼の故郷の古い記念碑である水車小屋を改修するにあたり、歴史的建築の内部を破壊するコンセプトを導き出した。すべては中央の大きな空白の舞台空間を中心に構成され、詩という物質性の不在をパフォーマンスや朗読によって劇場へと変換する試みを行う。ランボーが発した「私は別だ」という言葉のように、美術館の来場者は誰もが鑑賞者であり、鑑賞者は誰もが演者となる。

Parade

Des drôles très solides. Plusieurs ont exploité vos mondes. Sans besoins, et peu pressés de mettre en œuvre leurs brillantes facultés et leur expérience de vos consciences. Quels hommes mûrs ! Des yeux hébétés à la façon de la nuit d'été, rouges et noirs, tricolores, d'acier piqué d'étoiles d'or ; des faciès déformés, plombés, blêmis, incendiés ; des enrouements folâtres ! La démarche cruelle des oripeaux ! — Il y a quelques jeunes, — comment regarderaient-ils Chérubin ? — pourvus de voix effrayantes et de quelques ressources dangereuses. On les envoie prendre du dos en ville, affublés d'un luxe dégoûtant.

O le plus violent Paradis de la grimace enragée ! Pas de comparaison avec vos Fakirs et les autres bouffonneries scéniques. Dans des costumes improvisés avec le goût du mauvais rêve ils jouent des complaintes, des tragédies de malandrins et de demi-dieux spirituels comme l'histoire ou les religions ne l'ont jamais été. Chinois, Hottentots, bohémiens, niais, hyènes, Molochs, vieilles démences, démons sinistres, ils mêlent les tours populaires, maternels, avec les poses et les tendresses bestiales. Ils interpréteraient des pièces nouvelles et des chansons "bonnes filles". Maîtres jongleurs, ils transforment le lieu et les personnes et usent de la comédie magnétique. Les yeux flambent, le sang chante, les os s'élargissent, les larmes et des filets rouges ruissellent. Leur raillerie ou leur terreur dure une minute, ou des mois entiers.

J'ai seul la clef de cette parade sauvage.

Arthur Rimbaud's manuscript of *Les Illuminations* 「イリュミナシオン」アルチュール・ランボー自筆原稿 (1886)

Montage on the site　敷地へのモンタージュ

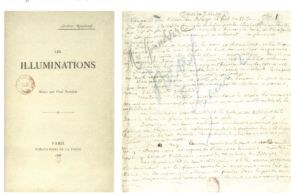

Les Illuminations　『イリュミナシオン』(1886)

Poésies complètes　『全詩集』(1895)

Ma bohème　『わが放浪』(1919)

A circle of witches　魔女の儀式 (1700)

T and O map　T-O マップ (7C)

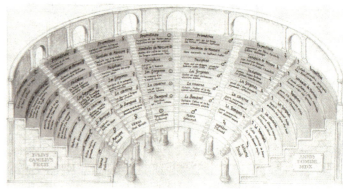

Theatre of Memory by Giulio Camillo　「記憶の劇場」ジュリオ・カミッロ (1511)

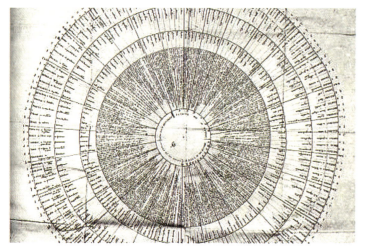

Memory System by Giordano Bruno　「記憶のシステム」ジョルダーノ・ブルーノ (1582)

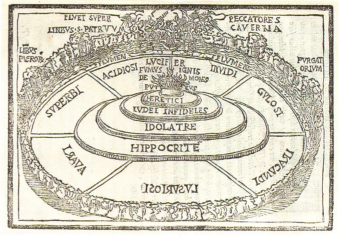

Hell and Paradise by Cosimo Rosselli　「天国と地獄の図」コジモ・ロッセリ (1579)

In Rimbaud's poetry space, the outcry of his soul, the destruction of meaning and violent emotions are so striking.
ランボーの詩の空間を考えていた。言葉の中に宿る、生命の叫び、意味の破壊、感情への暴挙、ランボーの過激さは衝撃だった。

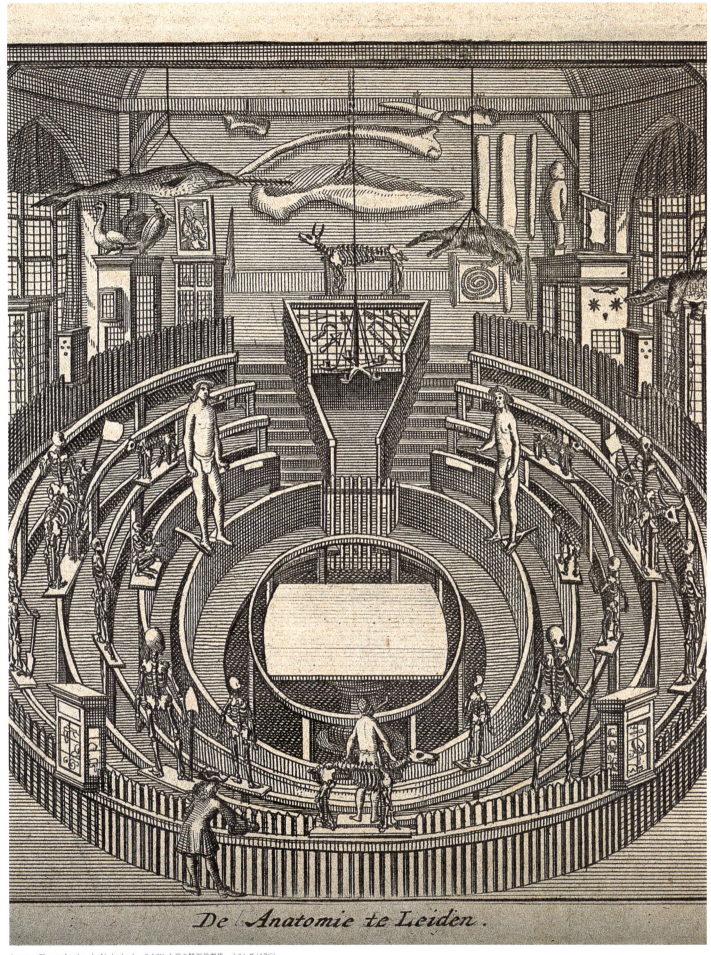

Anatomy Theatre, Leyden, the Netherlands　ライデン大学の解剖学劇場、オランダ (17C)

An amphitheater was a stage for drama but also a place for executions. It is formed by the actor-spectator accomplice relationship.
円形劇場はドラマの中心舞台であると同時に生と死の処刑場でもある。そこは演者と鑑賞者の共犯関係によって成り立っている。

Map of Charleville, France　シャルルヴィルの地図、フランス (1753)

Old watermill, Charleville (currently Arthur Rimbaud Museum)　現在ランボー記念館となっているシャルルヴィルの水車小屋 (1904)

Rimbaud at 17 years old　17歳のランボー (1872)

Coin de table by H.Fantin Latour 「テーブルの片隅」
H.ファンタン・ラトゥール (ランボー左から2番目) (1872)

The guests at the Hôtel de l'Univers, Yemen
オテルドルニバースにて (ランボー右から2番目)、イエメン (1879)

Map of Rimbaud in Ethiopia　ランボーのエチオピア行程図 (1926)

Letter to Izambard　イザンバールへの手紙 (1870)

Rimbaud in Harar　ハラールでのランボー (1883)

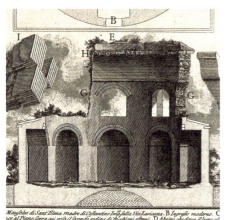
Saint Helen by G.B. Piranesi　「聖ヘレン」ピラネージ

Remnants of Roman ruins　ローマ遺跡の残骸

Grotta d'incanti by J. Vezzani　「エンチャントの洞窟」J. ヴェザーニ (1728)

Rimbaud's poetry was a revolution. His words rip our emotions and destroy meaning. We searched for spaces of passage and absence.
ランボーの詩は革命だった。詩が感情を切り裂き、言葉が意味を破壊するのなら、ランボー美術館は追憶と不在の建築にしたいと考えていた。

Concepturtal Collage　コンセプトコラージュ

In this space, visitors become actors. It is neither a museum nor a theater, but a space dedicated to Rimbaud's poetry.
この空間では来場者は鑑賞者でありながら演者となり、演者は一方で鑑賞者となる。美術館でも劇場でもない、ランボーの詩の空間。

Hirosaki Contemporary Art Museum

（仮称）弘前市芸術文化施設 ｜ Hirosaki, Japan 2017- ｜ museum competition, 1st prize, ongoing

The brick warehouses in Hirosaki,built during the Meiji period, were the first cider factory in Japan and have been an important part of the local landscape in Yoshino-cho for a long time. The brick warehouses, built of bricks specially developed to withstand severe snow conditions in the region, have gone through numerous additions and renovations over many years and most of them have been demolished and no longer exist. In Japan, there are very few cases of conversion and active utilization of historic buildings as contemporary cultural facilities, and most of the historic buildings are doomed to be demolished due to their "oldness". Brick buildings, which cannot be built anymore due to various restrictions in Japan today, are an important lineage in Japanese architectural history and precious cultural heritage not to be demolished. The goal of historic building renovation, on the other hand, is not only the repair of old buildings. Renovation design of a historic building starts by verifying its historical significance and rebuildability as well as understanding its dignity and potential. In order to pass on the memory of these brick buildings to future generations, we are using bricks as much as possible to renovate them into contemporary brick structures. In addition, new cider gold-colored roofs, inspired from their history as the first cider factory in Japan, highlight the presence of a new cultural facility. In the interior, the existing floors are removed and structural reinforcements are applied to fully use the generous space in the warehouse and convert it into a space where visitors can take time to appropriate a site-and time- specific artwork.

明治時代に建てられた弘前の煉瓦倉庫を改修し現代アートの美術館をつくるプロジェクトである。弘前市吉野町の煉瓦倉庫群は、日本で最初のシードル（りんご酒）工場として長年この街の風景を支えてきた。厳しい雪国の中で、独自に煉瓦を開発してつくった煉瓦倉庫群は増築や改築を繰り返しながら、そのほとんどはすでに解体され時代とともに失われた。国内では近代文化遺産を保存だけでなく、現代文化として積極的に活用するような事例はまだ数少なく、大半は「古さ」を理由に取り壊される。国内では煉瓦造りによる建築は二度とつくられることのない貴重な建築の系譜であり、壊してはならない文化遺産でもある。一方、古い建物の改修とは直すことが目的ではない。建物の歴史性や再現不可能性を検証し、その建築の尊厳と可能性を知ることから設計が始まる。この煉瓦建築の記憶の継承を目的としていくために、あらゆる場所で煉瓦を多用し尽くして改修を行う現代煉瓦建築とした。また屋根は日本初のシードル工場にちなんでチタンによるシードルゴールドとすることにより新たな文化施設として未来の風景を映し出す。内部空間においては、倉庫がもつ大らかな空間を最大限活かすように、既存の床を抜き、耐震補強を行いながら、サイトスペシフィックとタイムスペシフィックをコンセプトとした現代アートと対峙する空間が設けられる。

Brick warehouses under construction in Hirosaki　弘前煉瓦倉庫の建設当時

Exterior of the brick warehouses　煉瓦倉庫外観

Apple farm and Mt.Iwaki in the early Meiji period　明治時代初期のりんご園と岩木山

The first brick factory in Japan　日本で最初の機械式煉瓦工場

Interior of B building in the Taisho period　大正時代のB棟内部

Hirosaki Aerial View (detailed view)　「弘前市鳥瞰図原画」（詳細）

Cider press　サイダーの圧搾機 (17C)

Wine barrels making process　ワイン樽の製作過程 (16C)

Beer brewing process　ビールの醸造過程 (16C)

Adam and Eve under the apple tree　りんごの木の下のアダムとイブ

Illustration of brick making　煉瓦製造図 (15C)

Gold extracted from Bendigo Goldfields　ベンディゴ金鉱産の金塊

Hirosaki was formed next to a castle surrounded by apple trees. The brick cider factory has been in the landscape for 100 years.
弘前は城下町である一方でりんごが街の風景をつくってきた。そこに近代産業が訪れ、日本初のシードル工場をつくり、100年続く風景を残した。

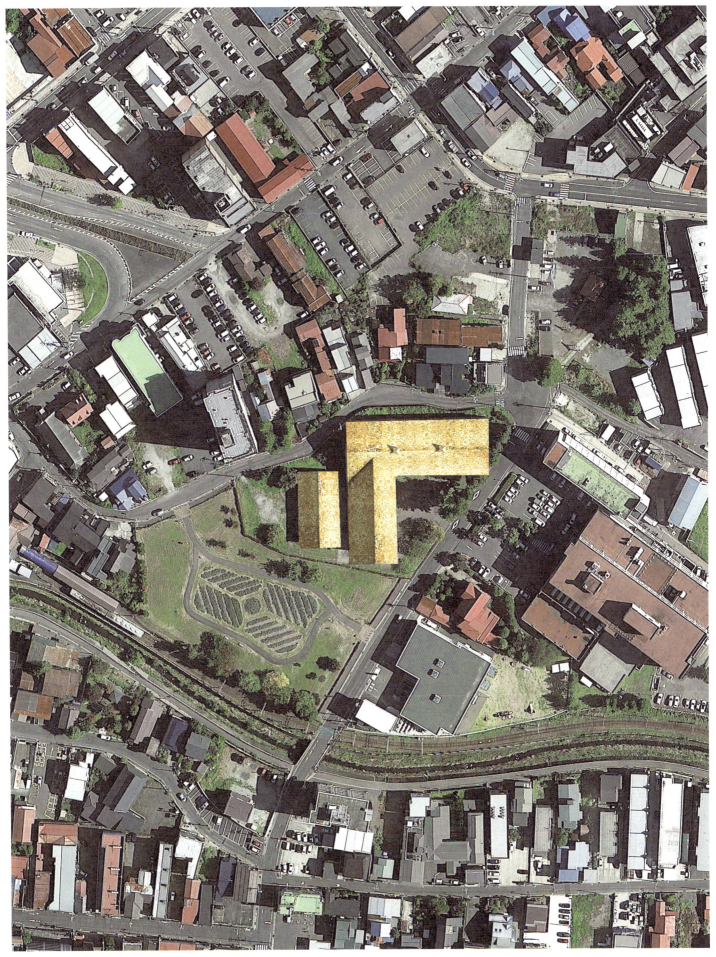

Montage on the site　敷地へのモンタージュ

For renovation projects, it is not about repairing broken parts but restoring what was lost.
改修計画は「何を直すか」から考えなくては意味がない。壊れたものを直すのではなく、失ったものを取り戻すことから始まる。

Detail photos of the site　現場詳細写真

They made their own bricks to build the warehouses. We explored further possibilities of building by observing traces of the past.
当時、煉瓦倉庫は煉瓦工場までつくり煉瓦を製造してこの建築をつくり上げた。度重なる改築や修復の痕跡から、この建築の可能性を探る。

The brick warehouse and the cider-gold roof will form a landscape in the future. A landscape of space and time.
煉瓦建築とシードルゴールドの屋根が未来の原風景をつくる。原風景とは空間的な風景だけではなく時間的な風景のことでもある。

Concept model　コンセプト模型

Shibuya Department Store

渋谷デパートメントストア ｜ Tokyo, Japan 2015 ｜ complex international competition, shortlisted

People have gathered various types of items from around the world to trade and do business at market places, as observed in historic examples including bazaars from the Mesopotamian civilization and West Asia, agorae and emporiums from Ancient Greece, and Trajan's Market from the Roman Empire. The origin of department stores goes back to the 19th century in the West. The interior of the first department store Le Bon Marché in Paris had a magnificent central atrium with shop floors around it, and this store style spread through major countries in the world. After the invention of electric light, illuminated window displays at department stores allowed for people to enjoy "window shopping" which became a typical night street view in big cities. In Shibuya, markets started and expanded from Washington Heights (the United States Armed Forces housing complex) after World War II. Since the 1970's, Shibuya has been the top runner of Tokyo's street culture disseminating the latest cultural trends to the world. A reconstruction project of a commercial facility was implemented with the aim of creating a new base for cultural promotion. We proposed an architecture design integrating the gently undulating valley topography and street culture of Shibuya into a three-dimensional form—in other words, we aimed to transform the city of Shibuya into an architectural form, rather than making a building. The interior space was planned in such a way that diagonal exterior and interior circulation paths keep intersecting at various points. Our challenge was to create an architecture representing the future of Shibuya by designing spaces based on the diagonal network system of the 21st century, which is neither the central atrium style of the 19th century nor the horizontal floor style of the 20th century.

「Market Place」は、メソポタミア文明や西アジアから広まったバザールや古代ギリシアのアゴラやエンポリウム、ローマ時代のトラヤヌスの市場などさまざまな文明によってつくられ、人びとは物を都市に集め、交易と商売を行ってきた。「Department Store」は19世紀の西洋に端を発し、パリのボンマルシェに見られるセントラルボイドの壮麗なる空間と各フロアを店舗が取り囲むような形式が世界主要国へと展開し、電気の発明とともにショーウィンドウが都市の夜の風景となる。渋谷は戦後のワシントンハイツから市場が発達し、1970年代以降からは東京のストリートカルチャーの最先端の街として新しい文化を常に発信し続けている。その渋谷に新しい文化発信の拠点をつくろうと商業施設を建て替えるための国際コンペが行われた。渋谷のなだらかな谷間の地形とストリートカルチャーがそのまま立体化していくような、ひとつの建物というよりも、渋谷の街がそのまま建物になるような建築を目指した。屋外と屋内から動線が斜めに交わり続けるように内部は計画され、19世紀型の垂直なセントラルボイドでもなく、20世紀型の水平なフロアスタイルでもなく、21世紀型の地形的な空間づくりを試み、それが最も未来の渋谷らしい建築となるよう挑戦した。

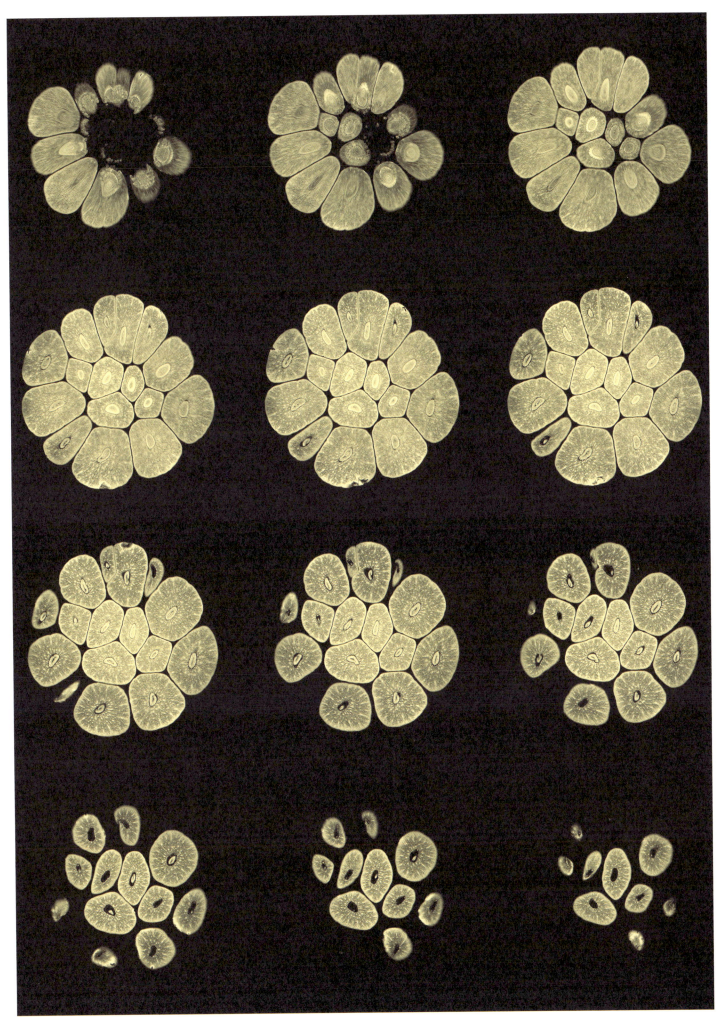

Serial images of MRI axial section of a bulb　MRIにより連続撮影された球根の断面図

Washington Heights, Shibuya　ワシントンハイツ、渋谷 (1954)

Aerial view around Shibuya station　渋谷駅周辺 (1952)

Market Scene by Pieter Aertsen　「市場の風景」ピーテル・アールツェン (1550)

The Effects of Good Government by A.Lorenzetti　「善政の効果」A.ロレンツェティ (1338)

Gum Department store, Moscow　グム百貨店、モスクワ (1893)

Grand Bazaar, Istanbul　グランドバザール、イスタンブール (1890's)

Window Shopping by T.Saylor　「ウィンドウショッピング」T.セイラー

Congestorium artificiose memoriae by Johannes Romberch
「記憶の場としての町」ヨハネ・ロンバーチ (1553)

The destruction of a Porphyrian Tree
ポルピュリオスの木の破壊 (1503)

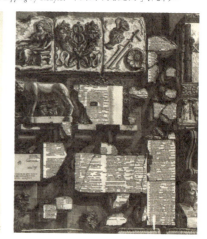
Lapides Capitolini Stones of the Capitol
ラピデ・カピトルニの石板図 (1762)

Development of Shibuya began from street culture. Markets have always been sources of lively energy, desires and dreams.
渋谷の始まりは市場から始まったストリートカルチャーである。マーケットの起源は都市に場所をつくり賑わいと欲と夢を与えてきた。

Nighttime in a City by Mir Sayyid 'Ali 「夜の街」ミールサイド・アリ (1540)

We discover new spatial styles from the past. The prototypes of the future may be found in the diversity of ancient spaces.
空間を形式は新しいだけでなく過去からも発掘可能である。古来の空間の多様性は、未来の空間を生き生きとさせる原型が潜んでいる。

Concept study models　コンセプトスタディ模型

Instead of a classic central atrium or modern flat floors, a diagonal sequence created an urban topography of space-scapes.
古典的な中央吹き抜けでもない、近代的な効率型のフロア構成でもない、斜めに連続する空間が都市的で、地形的で、現代的に思えた。

Shopping is a form of urban communication. We sought to generate an environment where spaces multiply like cell divide.
ショッピングは都市のコミュニケーションである。空間が細胞分裂をするような交流と交換の生成環境を考えようとしていた。

Concept model　コンセプト模型

Twin Towers in Kai Tak Development

カイタック・ツインタワー | Hong Kong, China 2017 | complex international competition, shortlisted

It was architect's dream to build the tallest building. The pursuit of height promoted technological advancement, and the invention of steel and elevators allowed buildings to go higher. People started increasing spatial volumes by constructing high-rise buildings due to soaring land values and thus the building height became prioritized over the significance of the place. The city of Hong Kong, with one of the largest ports in Asia, is directly influenced by current world affairs. Because most parts of the island are hilly land, many buildings have been constructed on small lots one after another as a result of economic growth accelerated by the increased trade, and as a result, Hong Kong has now become the "Asian New York", a densely built-up high-rise city. The 320-hectare site of the former Kai Tak airport, the first international airport in Hong Kong, is currently undergoing major urban re-development and there is a plan to build new twin towers at a node connecting the city center and the new Kai Tak district. Twin towers as a set of identical buildings tend to be viewed as a symbolic existence. In this twin towers project, the design brief requested us to present a vision for connecting the history and future of Hong Kong. In response, we proposed an architectural design where Hong Kong's building typologies, ranging from ancient fork houses before the British colonial period to the cluster of apartment buildings in Kowloon Walled City to the high-rise buildings developed in the urban context, are concentrated and integrated. The skyscraper rises like a city comprising an intermix of various Hong Kong building typologies in different time periods and scales, adequately expressing the future of Hong Kong.

建築にとって高さは夢だった。建築は高さを求め技術を開発し、鉄鋼とエレベーターの発明によって、より高さを追求することが可能になった。限られた土地の値段が高騰すると、建築は高層化し、空間の量を増やし、場所の意味よりも高さが意義をもつようになった。香港はアジアの重要な港であり、世界の動きが直接都市に影響を与える。島の大半は丘陵地であるため限られた土地に高密度な建設が繰り返され、急速な交易により急激な成長を遂げたアジアのニューヨークのようでもある。香港最初の国際空港であったKai Tak（啓徳）国際空港跡地の約320haの土地が開発され、香港中心部とKai Tak地区を結ぶ結節点に新たなツインタワーが計画された。ツインタワーは同類の建物が並列することでシンボリックな存在になりがちであるが、本プロジェクトでは、香港の歴史と未来をつなぐビジョンが要求されていた。そこでイギリス占領時代以前の古民家から九龍城の住居群、そこから発展した香港の高層ビル群までの香港の建築のタイポロジーを一気に圧縮して一体化するような建築を考えた。無関係な時代と無関係なスケールが混在し同居する香港建築群がツインタワーとして都市のように聳え立つ風景が香港の未来にふさわしく思えた。

Docks and harbor from the cliffs, Hong Kong　崖より港を望む、香港 (1873)

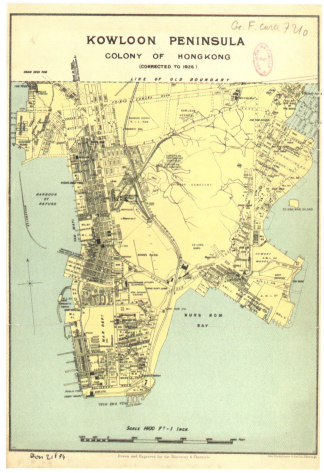
Map of Kowloon Peninsula, Hong Kong　九龍半島地図, 香港 (1926)

Yau Ma Tei Harbor　油麻地碼頭 (1880)

Kai Tak Airfield　啓徳空港 (1930)

Kowloon Walled City　九龍城砦 (1989)

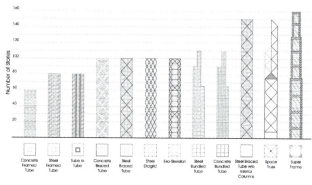
The graph of the number of floors and structures　高層ビルの階数と外部構造の関係 (2007)

Medieval Castle Section　中世の城図 (1885)

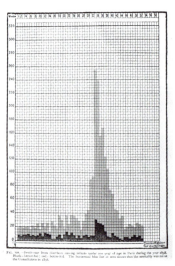
Overlapped graph　重ね合わされたグラフ

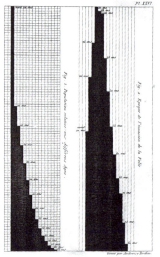
Paralleled graphs　並列に比較されたグラフ

Optical micrograph　光学顕微鏡によるミクロ写真

Hong Kong rapidly developed. Desire and chaos in the world intersected, and urban dreams materialized into towers on the island.
香港の歴史は交易による急成長の歴史でもある。世界の欲望と混沌がこの島で交わり、限られた土地の中で都市の理想を高層化させ続けていった。

Hong Kong architecture collage　香港建築のコラージュ

Hong Kong building typologies, from ancient houses to towers are integrated. Contradictions characterize the city.
香港の古い民家から新しい高層タワーまでをひとつの建築にできないかと考えた。矛盾を抱え突き進むことが最も香港らしい建築に思えた。

Concept study models　コンセプトスタディ模型

How high can a building go? Architecture, in an endless quest for height, elevates technologies and people's desires.
建築はどこまで高く伸び続けることが可能か。建築は高さを求めて技術を開発し、高さは欲望によって建築をより高く成長させる。

Volume study models　ボリュームスタディ模型

Building twin towers is not about building two identical towers. Each tower adapts to its surroundings.
ツインタワーは同じタワーをふたつつくることではない。ふたつそれぞれが周辺環境に適合することで都市の一部となり、連動し始める。

Yokohama Station Department Store

（仮称）横浜駅デパートメントストア ｜ Yokohama, Japan 2016- ｜ interior design ongoing

Yokohama was the first port city in Japan to open its ports to foreign ships in 1859 prior to the opening of the country. Yokohama has served as a gateway to the world, and a center of exchange for foreign and domestic cultures, intermixing, eclectic combinations, and the advancement of various styles in different eras, have promoted growth and development of Yokohama's unique culture and future. Yokohama Station was one of the first railway stations that opened in 1872 when a railway was built between Shinbashi and Yokohama. Today, the average number of people using the station per day is 2.2 million, the fifth busiest in the world. There is a plan to build a new Yokohama Station building connected to the west exit, and we are designing the public spaces (common areas) from first to tenth floors in the entire commercial facility with a total floor area of approximately 21,000m². The station building has been under development for a long time, and we were requested to design the connection between "*ekinaka*" (inside a station) and "*machinaka*" (inside a city). While a commercial facility is a place used for a specific purpose, "*machi*" (city) is a public space where people walk around freely. In order to convert this building to *machi*, we are incorporating maps of "global port cities" that have connections with Yokohama as maps of the interior spaces. Each floor is based on a map of a city and the interior space is entirely covered with a single material. Inspired from bricks, a characteristic material of Yokohama, we are designing interior spaces covered with tiles from around the world; conveying the stories of each port city.

横浜は1859年に開国へ向けて日本で初めて開かれた港町である。横浜から世界へつながり、異国の文化と自国の文化が交換され、さまざまな時代様式の混在と折衷と発展が、これまでの横浜の文化と未来を育んできた。横浜駅は同様に1872年に日本で初めて新橋・横浜間を開通した鉄道駅であり、現在は1日平均220万人と世界で5番目に利用者数の多い駅である。そこに新たな西口と連結した横浜駅ビルが建ち上がり、地上1階から10階までのYokohama Station Department Storeのパブリックスペース、延べ床面積約21,000m²のデザインを行うことになった。ここでは駅ビルとして長年計画されていた「エキナカ」と「マチナカ」をつなぐデザインが求められた。商業施設は目的性が高い建物でありながら、「マチ」は自由に人が歩き回るパブリックスペースである。そこで建物の内部を「マチ」へと変換するために、横浜とつながりのある「世界の港マチ＝グローバルポートシティ」を研究し、各都市の「マチ」の特性を探りながら建物の内部へと展開した。各フロアはそれぞれのマチの地図によって構成され、空間全体をオリジナルデザインのタイルで覆い尽くす。明治期から続く横浜の煉瓦から想起した世界中のタイルで包まれる物語性のある空間となる。

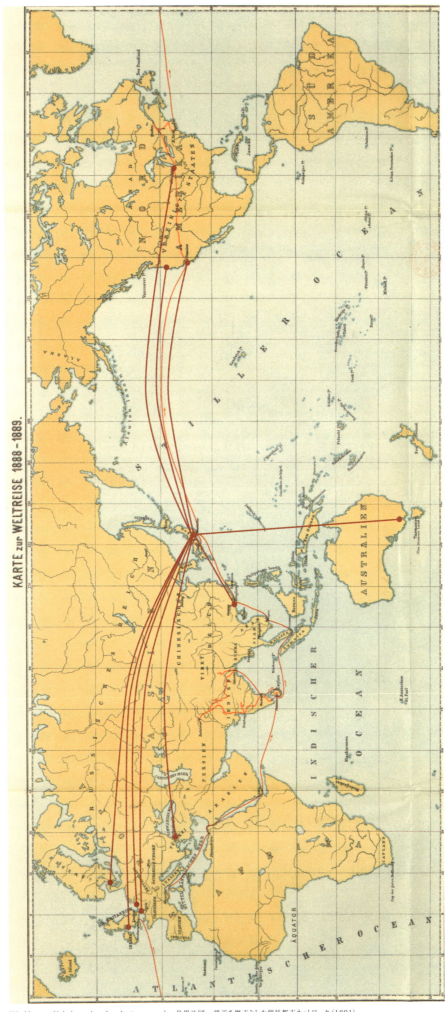

World map・Yokohama-based trade city network 　世界地図・横浜を拠点とした貿易都市ネットワーク (1891)

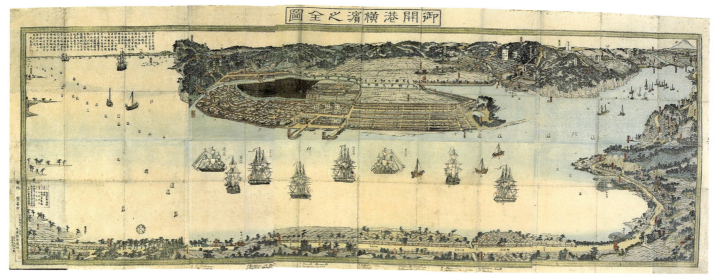
Complete Picture of the Opened Port of Yokohama by Utagawa Sadahide 「御開港横浜之全図」歌川貞秀 (1859)

Steam Train at Yokohama seashore by Utagawa Hiroshige III 「横浜海岸鉄道蒸気車図」三代目歌川広重 (1874)

General seaside view of Yokohama 横浜海岸部 (1880's)

Waterford, Ireland ウォーターフォード、アイルランド (1890's)

Istanbul, Turkey イスタンブール、トルコ (1905)

Chicago, U.S. シカゴ、アメリカ (1941)

World Map drawn based on a voyage survey by Cantino カンティノによる航海調査をもとに描かれた世界地図 (1502)

Egyptian paintings エジプトの装飾 (1832)

Yokohama is Japan's first port opened to the world. The port promoted cultural and political exchanges that aimed towards the future.
日本で最初に開港した横浜港。横浜から世界の港へとつながり、文化と歴史が入り混じり始め、時代は不可逆な未来へと向かっていく。

Mediaeval tiles from Chertsey Abbey　チャーツィー修道院のタイル (1858)

When a single entity is fragmented or fragments are integrated a new relationship is formed. Meanings transform into memories.
ひとつのものがばらばらになり、ばらばらのものがひとつになると、そこには新たな関係が生まれる。断片は意味となり、意味は記憶へと変貌する。

Grobal Port City Map Collage　グローバルポートシティマップコラージュ
The drawings are in preliminary phase and are different from actual plans (including drawings on pages 290-293)
掲載の図版は検討段階であり実際とは異なります。(290-293ページの図面も含む)

Maps of global port cities are superimposed on each floor of the Yokohama department store.
各階のフロアに都市の地図を埋め込む。グローバルポートシティ（世界の港町）が横浜駅デパートメントのフロアマップとなる。

Concept model　コンセプト模型

Tiles are used in many civilizations in the world. Different tiles create a variety of spaces of richness and diversity.
タイルは古代よりさまざまな文明によってつくられてきた。さまざまなタイルの断片が集まり、多様な空間が多様なまま混在する空間を目指している。

Chiso Building

千總本社ビル | Kyoto, Japan 2017- | renovation ongoing

Chiso is one of the oldest kimono makers in Kyoto founded in 1555 under the name Chikiriya. Chiso has kept its tradition alive for a long time: it started out as a Buddhist monks' vestment maker in the Muromachi period, developed the Yuzen dying technique in the Edo period, and have been making kimonos for the Imperial family since the Meiji period. Yuzen is a dyeing technique of directly hand-painting patterns on while silk, unlike most fabric making techniques of weaving dyed threads. Chiso has been pursuing the beauty of kimono by producing kimonos celebrating the beauty of the four seasons and formal kimonos for ceremonial occasions using the Yuzen dying technique. In general, Japanese aesthetics tend to focus on "modest beauty" represented by the concept of "*wabi*" and "*sabi*." On the contrary, the other side of Japanese aesthetics, which may be described as "abundant beauty", developed over a long time from within the cultures of the Heian period, the Momoyama period, and the Edo period. It conceived rich expressions of "kabi" (splendor) and "miyabi" (elegance) based on complex and elaborate aesthetic values, which may be equivalent to the Baroque culture in the West. For this project, we are planning an addition and renovation of the current headquarters completed in 1989 and converting the floors from the basement to the second floor into a headquarters for Kyoto Yuzen. We are also planning new spaces accommodating a "*wa*" salon, "*monozukuri*" workshop, and a gallery contributing to shaping the future of Japanese culture, as well as promoting Yuzen kimonos.

千總は1555年以来、京都を拠点に千切り屋一門として始まった着物の老舗である。室町では法衣商、江戸時代には「京友禅」の技術を開発し、明治時代からは皇室へ着物を誂えるなど長年にわたって伝統を継承し続けている。友禅とは糸に染色して織り込む布づくりではない。純白の絹地に直接絵付けを行い、柄を合わせて着物へと仕立てる、世界に類を見ない友禅の技法によって「美」を表現し続けてきた。通常、日本の美は「わび・さび」に象徴されるように禅なる美意識として「簡素な美」へと認識が向かいがちである。しかし、日本のもうひとつの美として「かび（華美）・みやび（雅）」なる表現は、桃山文化や江戸文化によって培われた豊饒なる美であり、「日本のバロック」として多様なる美意識として表現されてきた。1989年に京都三条通りに建てられた千總ビルはその建物全館を千總の本社と本舗として増築と改築を行う計画となる。千總の460年の歴史を基盤に友禅着物だけでなく、和サロン、ものづくり、ギャラリーなど和文化の伝統と未来を担うプロジェクトとして進行している。

Chikirika no zu 「千切花の図」(1915)

Nishimura Sozaemon south shop in the Meiji period
西村總左衛門南店、明治期

Chiso Company building　株式会社千總商店洋式社屋 (1937)

North facade of the current Chiso Foundation building
現在の千總本社北側正面

Kyuko zufu　『織物　求古図譜』(19C)

Kyuko zufu　『織物　求古図譜』(19C)

Kyuko zufu　『織物　求古図譜』(19C)

Hem of a kimono shown in the woodprint
版画にみられる着物裾部分 (19C)

Sleeve of a kimono shown in the woodprint
版画にみられる着物袖部分 (19C)

Adoration of the Magi by Peter Paul Ruben
「三王礼拝」ピーテル・パウル・ルーベンス (1617)

Virgin of Carmel by Diego Quispe Tito
「カルメルの聖母」ディエゴ・クスペ・テイト (17C)

Mitsui Echigoya at Suruga-chō by Utagawa Toyoharu　「浮絵駿河町呉服屋図」歌川豊春 (1768)

The Gallery of Cornelis van der Geest　「コーネルス・ファン・デル・ジェーストの画廊」(1628)

Chiso represents the history of kimonos. The beauty of kimonos or the "Japanese Baroque" may be similar to European Baroque.
千總の歴史は和装の歴史である。着物の華美なる艶やかさは「和のバロック」であり、同時代の「洋のバロック」との近似性と同調性が見え隠れする。

茶の湯が簡素な「わび・さび」ならば、着物は「かび（華美）・みやび（雅）」であり、豊穣なる美の追求もまた和の美意識の根源である。

Chiso's Yuzen kimono *Noshimon Kyoyuzen*　千總友禅「熨斗文友禅染」(2015)

Tea ceremony represents simplicity or "wabi" and "sabi", kimonos seek diversity or "kabi"and "miyabi" in Japanese aesthetics.
茶の湯が簡素な「わび・さび」ならば、着物は「かび（華美）・みやび（雅）」であり、豊穣なる美の追求もまた和の美意識の根源である。

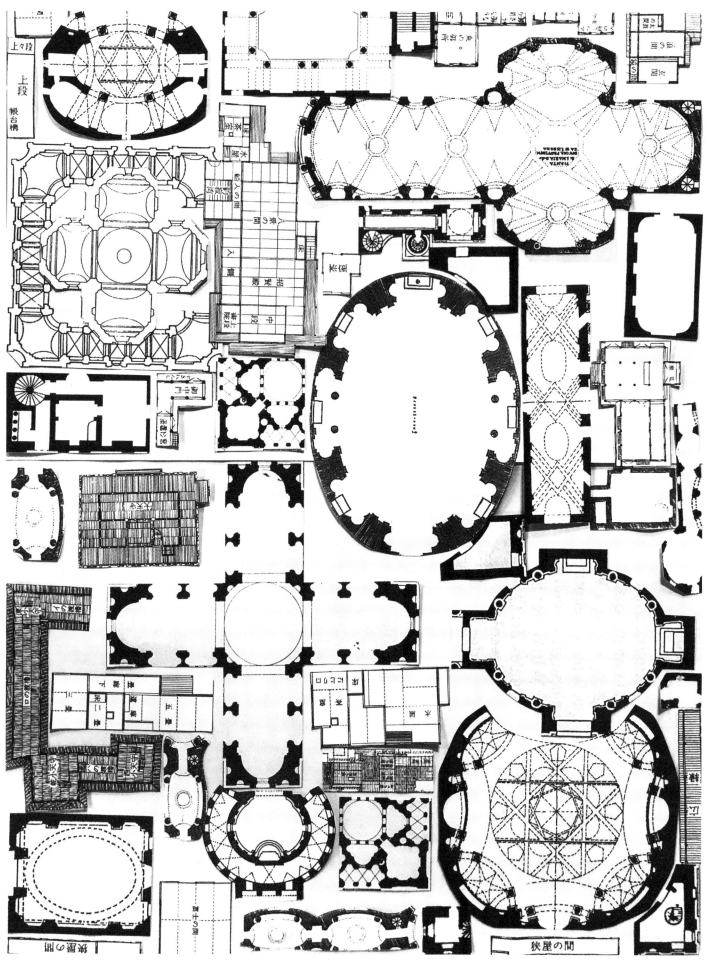

Concept plan collage　コンセプト平面コラージュ

Examining the 17th-19th century Japanese and Western Baroque spaces, focusing on diversity and transformation of spaces.
17-19世紀の「和と洋のバロック」空間を研究する。バロックの建築空間は形式ではない、様式の多様性と変容を考察していく。

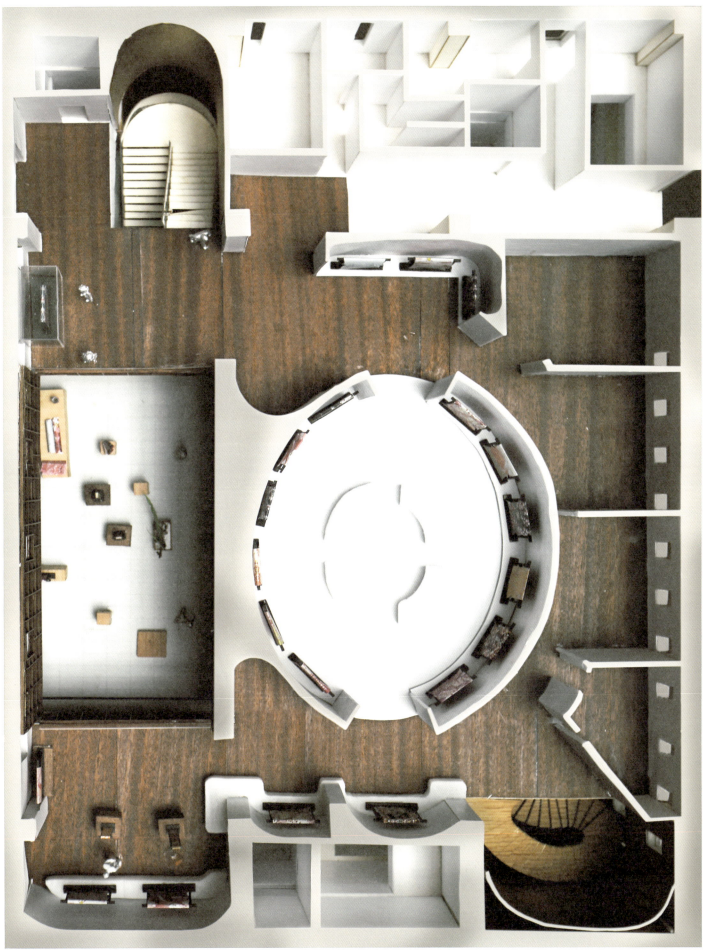

Study model　スタディ模型

A soft space is inserted into a hard space. Spaces start blending into one another when an incongruous space intervenes.
かたい空間にやわらかな空間を挿入していく。矛盾した空間が入ることで、空間は溶け合いひとつになり始める。

A House for Oiso

A House for Oiso | Kanagawa, Japan 2014-15 | house completed

Oiso is one of the oldest inhabited areas in this region, where people had lived for more than 3,500 years, since the Late Jomon period. This area is surrounded by sacred mountains including Koma-yama, and *kofun-gun* (tumulus clusters) where ancient ruins still exist. In the Early Modern period, Oiso was one of the most popular resting spots along the route connecting Edo and Kyoto. During the Showa era, it was a popular resort area and many villas were built. But in recent years, daily life in Oiso, blessed with beautiful landscapes and the dignity of the place passed down since the ancient times, is being lost due to residential land development in the area. We conducted research on dwellings from the ancient period to the premodern period and conceived an idea of building a house integrating characteristic elements/styles of each era, namely a pit dwelling from the Jomon period, raised floor dwelling from the Yayoi period, dug-standing pillars from the Medieval period, *machiya* (townhouse) from the Edo period, and villa from the Showa period. Our intention was to build a Japanese house that Japan had forgotten. This project was named "House for Oiso" meaning that the house is built for the place, and not "House in Oiso" meaning that the house is built in the place. A house is not only a place where a family spends its daily life, but fundamentally a place where a family always comes back and sleep. Our intention was to build a house which originated in the past and will remain standing in the future by digging into distant memories of the place, instead of simply imagining a new future house.

大磯は3500年以上前の縄文時代後期頃から人の暮らしが途絶えることのなかった地域であった。この地域は古くから高麗山などの霊山に囲まれ、古墳群や遺跡が未だに残っている。その一方で、近世には江戸と京都を結ぶ宿泊処の名所となり、昭和の時代には別荘地として邸宅建築が建てられた地域でもある。昨今、この地域の分譲開発によって、風光明媚な大磯の暮らしと古代から受け継がれてきた場所の尊厳が失われつつあった。そこで前近代までの住居研究を行い、縄文＝竪穴、弥生＝高床、中世＝掘立柱、江戸＝町家、昭和＝邸宅を統合したひとつの家、日本が忘れた日本の家、そんな家をつくりたいと思った。家とは家族が生活のために暮らす場所であるだけではなく、家族が眠りに帰る場所が本来の家なのである。新しい未来の家を夢見るよりも、遠い場所の記憶を掘り返すことで未来へと残せるような家をこの場所につくりたいと思っていた。そしてこのプロジェクトを家が土地の上に建つ「House in Oiso」ではなく、家が場所のために建つ「A House for Oiso」と名付けることとした。

Thatched cottages in Japan 茅葺の民家 (1868)

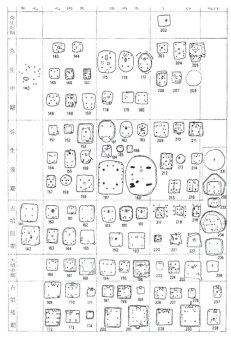
Classification table of Japanese ancient houses　弥生・古墳時代における住居一覧表

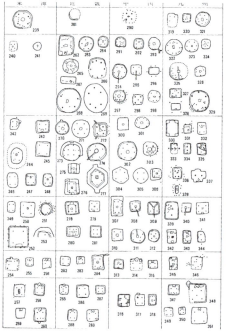

Map of Kita-Kamakura, Japan　北鎌倉の地図 (1685)

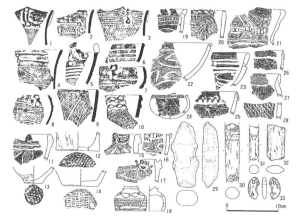
Relics of the late Jomon period, Takanezawa Town　縄文時代後 - 晩期の遺物、高根沢町

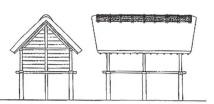
Pit dwelling　堅穴建物 (復元図)

Restoration drawing of East Festival Stage　東祭殿 (復元図)

Defensive tower　物見櫓 (復元図)

Kamaguchi Tomb near Oiso before the surrounding area was developed
大磯町近郊にある釜口古墳

National Highway No. 1 in Oiso during the Meiji period
国道1号本町通り、大磯町 (明治時代)

Rakuchu rakugai zu byobu by Kano-ha in the Late Muromachi period
「洛中洛外図屏風」狩野派 (室町時代末期)

Tokaido-53tsugi Oiso Toragaishi by Katsushika Hokusai
東海道五十三次「大磯 虎ヶ石」葛飾北斎 (1802)

Tokaido-53tsugi Oiso Toragaame by Utagawa Hiroshige
東海道五十三次「大磯 虎ヶ雨」歌川広重 (1833)

Toueikan hanei no zu by Utagawa Kuniasda III
「祷龍館繁栄之図」三代目歌川国貞 (1891)

People have lived in Oiso for 3500 years. All the Japanese house typologies from pit dwellings to modern villas are embedded.
大磯は3500年以上前から人が住み始めた。竪穴式、高床式、掘立柱、町家、邸宅式の日本の住居形式のすべてがこの場所に記憶されている。

Craters on the moon　月面クレーター (1863)

Excavation is a way of discovering spaces. Excavation of a place is the beginning of architecture and its spaces.
掘ることは空間の発見である。場所を掘ることが建築の始まりであり、空間の始まりである。

Sketch　スケッチ

To sketch is to add images on a piece of paper. Intangible images become perceivable and gradually materialize into architecture.
スケッチは白紙にイメージを与えていく。見えなかったイメージが意識化され、スケッチを描き続けることでイメージは建築へと近づいていく。

When architecture becomes a "home", it is a place to come back to. A house is architecture for sleeping.
建築が家になるとき、そこは帰る場所となる。家族が安心して眠りに帰る場所。家は建築における「眠りの場所」である。

Concept model　コンセプト模型

Todoroki House in Valley

Todoroki House in Valley | Tokyo, Japan 2017-18 | house completed

Todoroki Valley is a valley of the wind. The valley is situated among deep forest in the city. The ground surface is humid with flowing spring water, while valley winds constantly blow through the sky above. We focused on the unique environmental characteristics of "dry" and "wet" and conducted research on primitive dwellings in wetlands and drylands in the world. Architectural styles influenced by opposite environmental characteristics of "dry" and "wet" are composed of external elements determined by the climate and internal elements based on daily life. By integrating architectural styles rooted in completely different environments into a single building, we aimed to build architecture that does not belong to any particular time or place. The site is a residential lot situated in the densely built-up residential area, but it was originally surrounded by deep forests in the valley. We started to think about possible ways of developing forests again along with the construction of this house. Our aim was to build architecture of the future surrounded by deep forests where all living things — the house, plants and trees, and people — live happily and feel various aspects of life from a primal feeling of living below ground to a feeling of urban complexity resulting from vertically stacked spaces.

等々力渓谷は風の谷である。深い森の中の渓谷は、湧き水が出るなど地盤面の湿度は高く、上空では常に谷間からの風が吹き抜ける都会の森である。この渓谷の環境的特性である「DRY」と「WET」に着目し、世界中の湿地帯と乾燥地帯にある原始住居の研究を行った。「DRY」と「WET」という相反する環境的特性が生み出した建築の形式は、気候という外的要素と生活という内的要素から成り立ち、そのまったく異質な環境から生まれた建築をひとつに接合することで、どの時代のどの地域にも属さないような建築をつくろうとした。一方で敷地周辺は住宅が過密に建て込まれ、区画整備された都会の分譲地である。しかし、本来この場所は渓谷の深い森で覆われていたため、失われた森を取り戻すように、建築をつくりながら再び森をつくることは可能かと考え始めた。大きな森に覆われながら、地面の中に埋もれる原始的な居心地、空間が立体化され積み重なっていく都市的な複雑さと、それらすべてが渾然一体となり、家も植物も森も生活も生きとし生けるものすべてが生き生きと暮らせるような都会の未来の家を目指していた。

Chicken coop to protect from predators, Italy　捕食動物から守るための鶏小屋、イタリア (1926)

Aru Island House, Indonesia　アル島伝統住居、インドネシア

Malaysian Grave　首長の墓、マレーシア

House on the water, Philippines　水上住居、フィリピン

Kraal hut, South Africa　村落の小屋、南アフリカ

Cyprus House on the slope　キプロスの斜面住宅

House of boulders, Sudan　岩の家、スーダン

Hexagonal Wardian Case
六角形型ウォードの箱 (1800's)

Dome-shaped Wardian Case
ドーム型ウォードの箱 (1852)

Cultivation of Artemisia Absinthium
ニガヨモギの栽培 (809)

Cultivation of Ruta plants　ヘンルーダの栽培 (809)

Cultivation of palms in a greenhouse　温室内でのヤシの栽培 (1856)

Geographical distribution of vegetation　植生の地理的分布図 (1848)

The collection of Rohdea japonica by Sekine Untei　「小不老草名寄」関根雲停 (1832)

Architecture is built in an environment. An environment can be created by architecture. Architecture and the environment coexist.
建築は環境の中に建つ。環境から建築をつくることも、建築によって環境がつくられることもある。建築と環境は常に共存関係している。

Archaeological Research　アーキオロジカルリサーチ

Exploring primitive houses in drylands and wetlands. The future of environments and architecture is full of potential.
世界のWET（湿地帯）とDRY（乾燥地帯）の原始住居を研究し、環境と建築の密接な関係を探る。環境と建築の未来はまだ可能性に満ちている。

Concept study models　コンセプトスタディ模型

Ideas are born when working by hand. Hands produce the creative process. Models are not architecture but ideas of architecture.
発想は手でつくるところから生まれる。手からモノを生み出し、モノから創造が始まる。模型は建築ではない。建築のアイデアが模型なのである。

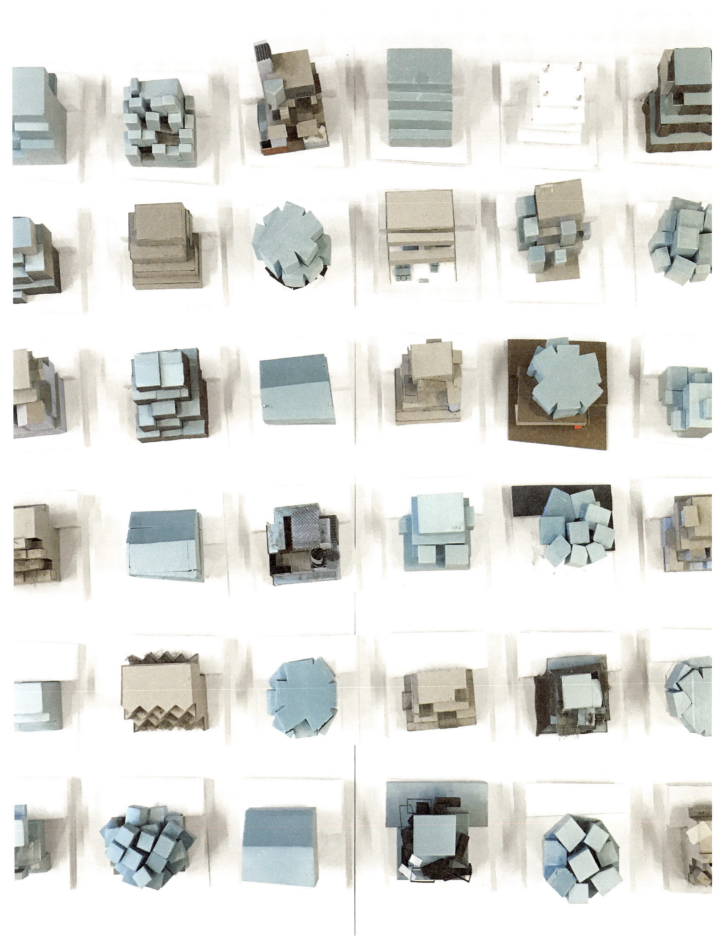

Concept study models　コンセプトスタディ模型

Similarity, difference, irregularity, peculiarity, ingenuity, and banality observed in models clarifying further possibilities.
模型を整然と並べる。そこから建築の相似、近似、差異、異形、変形、奇形、傑作、凡作、駄作、そしてその先の可能性が見えてくる。

Weekend House in Fontainebleau

フォンテーヌブロー週末住宅 ｜ Fontainebleau, France 2017- ｜ house ongoing

In the 9th century B.C. the Forest of Fontainebleau had been inhabited by an ancient civilization and some remains of primitive dwellings still exist around the forest here. Later, large numbers of trees had been continuously cut down to produce building materials and firewood. During the reign of Louis XIV, 80% of the forest had been felled and converted into farmland. In the 18th century, People planted trees to restore the shrinking forest and increase the amount of firewood, and later large numbers of pine trees were planted by Napoleon I. The Forest of Fontainebleau was designated as the world's first nature reserve in 1872. We are designing a weekend house in this expansive forest on land that was discovered by a pilot. Several weekend houses were built in the open areas of the forest in the 1960's. Our project site is located at the far end of this land, with a panoramic view of a 2000-hectare forest and valley that makes one imagine the edge of the earth. To build architecture in a forest is to return to the origin of architecture. An organic relationship between architecture and forest is indispensable to the life of the forest: architecture protects life from nature, while connecting life with nature. In terms of design conditions, we needed to think about a way to use the large site while coping with restrictions imposed upon designated nature reserves. For this weekend house where a family will spend special time away from daily life, we started studying design ideas about spaces and time with a focus on the sense of scale and distance between architecture, forest and surrounding landscape.

フォンテーヌブローの森はかつて紀元前9世紀頃より古代人が住み、森の周りには居住地を構えた原始住居の痕跡が残る。その後、この森ではパリの建設資材や熱源として大量の樹木が切り続けられ、ルイ14世の時代には森林の80%が伐採され、農地へと開拓された。失われ続ける森と燃料源を補うことを目的として、18世紀には再び森林を回復するための植林が行われ、ナポレオン1世によって大量の松が植えられた。その特異な自然の風景と背景により、フォンテーヌブローの森は1872年、世界で初めて自然保護地区として指定される。その広大な森の中に小さな別荘を計画している。この敷地はある飛行士によって発見され、森の隙間の開けた土地には、1960年代に数軒の別荘が建てられていた場所である。その最も奥に位置する敷地の先には約2,000haの森と谷間があり、地球の果てを見るような広大な森林の風景が広がる。森の中に建築をつくることは、建築の原点に立ち返ることであり、自然から生活を守り、自然とともに暮らす、建築と森林との柔らかな関係性によって成立する。広大な敷地と森と周囲の風景とのスケールと距離感を探りながら、週末住宅として非日常を過ごす空間と時間のアイデアを模索し始めた。

Spruce and pine forest 針葉樹林 (1908)

Map of Fontainebleau　フォンテーヌブローの地図 (1729)

Meeting of Napoleon and Pope Pius VII at Fontainebleau by A.H.Dunouy
「ナポレオン1世とピウス7世の対面」A.H.デュノー (1804)

The Very Rich Hours of the Duke of Berry
「ベリー公のいとも豪華なる時祷書」(1485)

Medieval hunting manual　中世の狩猟手引書 (1405)

Work in the forest　森林での作業 (16C)

Italian Garden at Villa Petraia　ペトライア荘のイタリア式庭園 (1599)

Château de Rueil　リュエイル城 (17C)

Maisons-Laffitte　メゾン・ラフィット (1838)

Forest of Fontainebleau　フォンテーヌブローの森 (1923)

The Edge of the woods, near Rambouillet　森の片隅、ランボワレット近郊

The Forest of Fontainebleau is as a natural reserve. We are studying its history involving the monarchy, hunting, and villas.
フォンテーヌブローの森は世界で最初の自然保護地区となった人工の森である。王国と森と狩りの歴史、そして森の中に建つ別荘の起源を探る。

History of Fontainebleau　フォンテーヌブローの森の岩 (1885)

Rare shaped rocks are scattered in the deep forest valley. We explore the relationship between rock formations and the landscape.
フォンテーヌブローの森の深い谷間には岩が散在している。岩は森とは異なる物質であり、その造形と風景の関係を探り始めた。

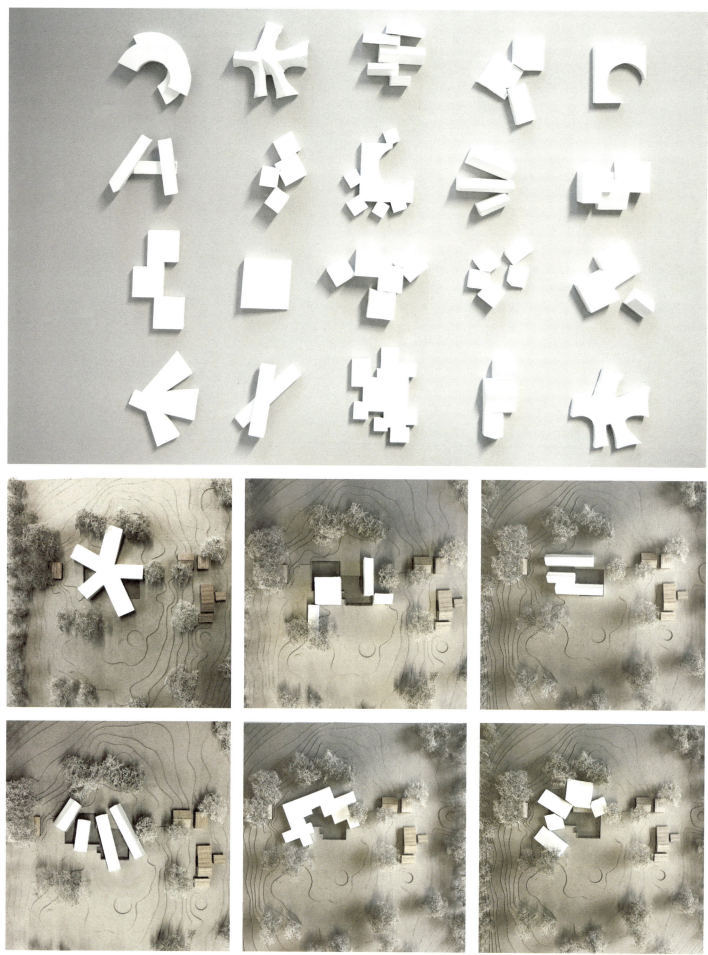

Concept study models　コンセプトスタディ模型

Architecture in a forest is different from architecture in a city. How can architecture exist in nature and become part of it?
森の中の建築は都市の中の建築とは異なる。建築が自然の中に建つことと、建築が自然になることを模索していた。

Concept model　コンセプト模型

A villa in the forest. Exploring the relationship between architecture and nature where many things are scattered in the landscape.
フォンテーヌブローの森の中に別荘をつくる。それはひとつの形ではなく、多数の固まりが風景の中に投げ出される森と建築の関係を考えている。

Toraya Paris

とらやパリ店 | Paris, France 2015 | interior design completed

"Tradition is a succession of innovations."
TORAYA, one of the oldest Japanese confectionery makers founded in Kyoto in the 16th century during the Muromachi period, has been passing down their tradition and spirit through generations while successively implementing innovations responding to each era. TORAYA Paris, which opened in 1980 on Rue Saint-Florentin between Rue Saint-Honoré running through the city center and Place de la Concorde, is the company's one and only overseas store. In 2015, they decided to renovate the store in celebration of the 35th anniversary of TORAYA Paris, to hand over the business to the next generation. Upon starting the project, TORAYA's 17th President Mitsuhiro Kurokawa requested us to create "a place to foresee TORAYA's tomorrow and new challenges." Japanese confectionary is basically made, packaged, and delivered to the customer entirely by hand. Therefore, traces of hand work are evident in the ingenious details of its taste, shape, and technique, which constitute the beauty of Japanese confectionery. Following TORAYA's tradition of making confectionery with only local ingredients, we conceived an idea of creating a Japanese-style space with only French building materials. All corners in the store are rounded to create a space where people feel softly wrapped inside the envelope, all made by hand using wood, stone, plaster, and steel.

「伝統は革新の連続である」。16世紀の室町時代に京都で創業した「とらや」は 歴史ある和菓子の老舗として伝統の精神を世代を超えて継承しながらも、その時代に合わせて未来への革新を繰り返してきた。1980年にパリの中心地、サントノレ通りからコンコルド広場へと抜けるサンフローランタン通りにできた「とらやパリ店」は、日本国外にある唯一の店舗である。2015年、オープン35周年を記念してパリ店は、次の世代に引き継ぐためにも店舗の改装を行うことにした。虎屋十七代当主、黒川光博社長より「新しい挑戦、明日のとらやを予見する場所にしてほしい」と伝えられ、このプロジェクトは始まった。和菓子は菓子のつくり始めからつくり終わりまで、そしてお客様の手元に届けるまですべてが手から手へと伝わる「手仕事」で賄われる。そのため、すべての味や形や技術の工夫には手仕事の痕跡が残り、その美しさが和菓子の魅力を支えている。そこでとらやがその土地の素材を使って和菓子をつくるという伝統に習い、フランスの土地の素材を用いながら和の空間をつくることをコンセプトとした。店内全ての角をなくし、木・石・漆喰・真鍮などさまざまな手仕事が空間を柔らかく包み込み、家具から把手、照明からサイン計画まですべてをオリジナルでデザインした。

Japanese confectionery "Wagashi" of four seasons　季節の和菓子

97

Tokyo Kazoku gakkou Gakushuin Engkaizu by Hashimoto Chikanobu
「東京華族学校学習院宴会図」橋本周延 (1877)

The salon of Madame Geoffrin by Anicet Charles Gabriel Lemonnier
「ジョフラン夫人のサロン」アニセ・シャルル・ガブリエル・ルモニエ (1812)

Pastry making process　菓子製作工程 (14C)

Catalan medieval cuisine　中世カタルーニャにおける調理風景

The invention of sugar refinery technique　砂糖製造方法の発明

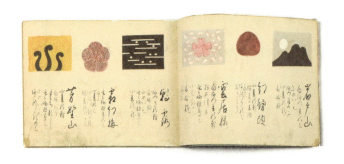

Drawing catalogue of Wagashi recipes　「御菓子之畫圖」(1707)

Drawing catalogue of new Wagashi recipes　「新製御菓子繪圖」(1824)

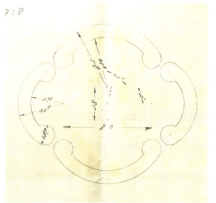

Drawing of emblem *Kantora*　〈鐶虎〉設計図

Wooden mold for wagashi　和菓子木型

Hinaseiro　雛井籠 (1776)

A study of the history of confectionery making and salon spaces. Japanese confectionery is entirely made by hand.
菓子を嗜む和と洋のサロン研究を行い、甘味の起源から菓子づくりの製造の歴史を辿る。和菓子はすべて手仕事によってつくられている。

甘味を嗜む場所は椅子とテーブルで決まる。とらやの「鐶虎」をモチーフに「Toraya chair」と「Yokan table」をデザインした。

Model of table and chairs　テーブルと椅子の模型

Chairs and tables are important elements at the salon. We designed "Toraya Chair" and "Yokan Table" using a motif of "Kantora."
甘味を嗜む場所は椅子とテーブルで決まる。とらやの「鐶虎」をモチーフに「Toraya chair」と「Yokan table」をデザインした。

Luce Tempo Luogo

Luce Tempo Luogo | Milan, Italy 2011 | installation completed

People have tried to find out what light is. Empedocles, Descartes, Galileo Galilei, Newton, Einstein, and many other scientists and researchers have been fascinated by light and made observations through numerous experiments. While light lets us see all physical entities, light itself cannot be perceived as one. When the sun shines or a light is turned on, we can see the light source but cannot see the light travelling through space between the source and the object. Nor can we see the light in its entirety even though the space is filled with light. For this art installation, we conducted various investigations and experiments with LEDs and developed ways to express the further possibilities of light. One of the unique properties of LEDs is the digitalization of light. In general, light emitted from incandescent lamps increases gradually and generates sine waveforms. On the other hand, LEDs have an extremely high response speed and we took advantage of this property to convert light into digital signals instead of waveforms and we developed programs for the lighting. We also developed a new light analyzing device; successfully reducing the light emission time down to 5/1,000,000 second. The light from this device, when illuminating flowing water, is seen as particles and creates points of light. On the other hand, by maximizing the light emission time to 2,000/1,000,000 second, the illuminated stream of flowing water appears as a line of light, instead of points. In this spatial installation, we visually expressed the "time" of light.

人類は光を知るために、エンペドクレスが、デカルトが、ガリレオ・ガリレイが、ニュートンが、アインシュタインが、そして名を馳せることのなかった多くの科学者や研究者が光に魅了され、実験と研究を重ね光の観測を行ってきた。光はすべての物質を可視化しているのに、光そのものを物質として見ることはできない。太陽が輝き、電気が発光するとその光源は可視可能ではありながら、光源から発せられた光が物質に届くまでの間の空間にも光はあり、光は空間を満たしながら、その光そのものを見ることはできない。ここではLEDの光のさまざまなリサーチと実験を行い、その可能性を引き出すインスタレーションを考えることとなった。LEDの特性のひとつは光をデジタル化することである。 通常、電球の光はサインカーブを描いて立ち上がる、一方、LEDの光の応答速度は、光をデジタル信号に変換し、波ではなく記号化することでプログラミングが可能となった。そこで新たに光の解析装置を開発し、発光時間を100万分の5秒まで縮め極小の光を水に投影して可視化することが可能となった。そして発光時間を100万分の2,000秒まで長く延ばすことで、光は点から線へと変わり、光の時間を可視化するインスタレーションが完成した。

THE ELEMENTS OF EUCLID.

BOOK I.

DEFINITIONS.

I.
A POINT is that which hath no parts, or which hath no magnitude.

II.
A line is length without breadth.

III.
The extremities of a line are points.

IV.
A straight line is that which lies evenly between its extreme points.

V.
A superficies is that which hath only length and breadth.

VI.
The extremities of a superficies are lines.

VII.
A plane superficies is that in which any two points being taken, the straight line between them lies wholly in that superficies.

VIII.
" A plane angle is the inclination of two lines to one another* in a plane, which meet together, but are not in the same direction."

IX.
A plane rectilineal angle is the inclination of two straight lines to one another, which meet together, but are not in the same straight line.

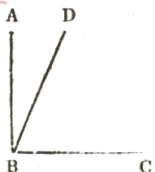

The definitious of the Elements of Euclid + Sketch　ユークリッド原論の定義＋スケッチ

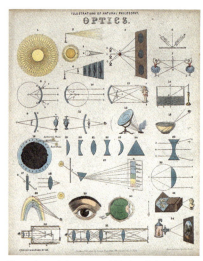
Forms of optical phenomena　光学現象一覧 (1850)

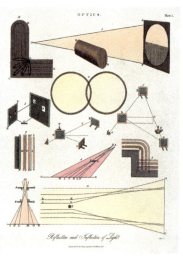
Forms of reflection and refraction
反射と屈折現象の一覧 (1819)

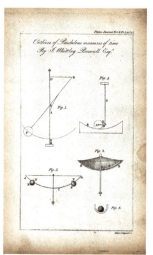
Diagrams of the double pendulum
二重振り子現象の解説図 (1809)

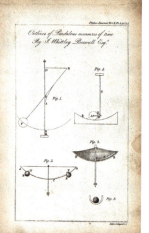
Graph showing the relationship between
tempo and pulse　拍数の関係図 (1890)

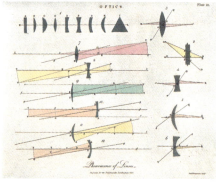
Diagrams of refraction of light　光の屈折解説図 (1920)

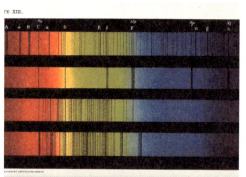
Optical spectra of stars　恒星の光学スペクトル

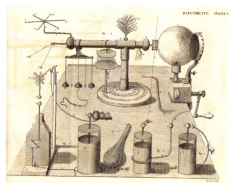
Electrical experiment apparatus　電気実験器具 (19C)

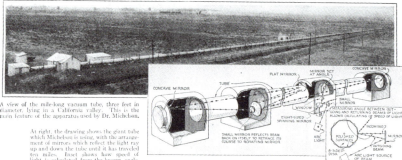
Michelson's measurement of the speed of light　マイケルソン干渉計による光速差実験 (1930)

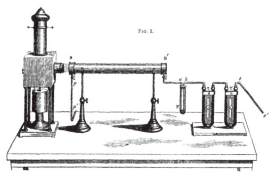
Tyndall's glass tube　チンダルが実験で用いたガラス管 (1879)

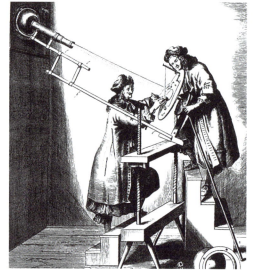
Observation of a solar eclipse　日食の観測 (1673)

"Philosophia" by R.Fludd　『フィロソフィア』R. フルド (1638)

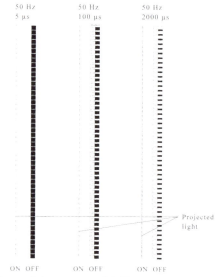
Diagram of light emission time　発光時間のダイアグラム

History of light observation. Light gives a form, and humans have made numerous efforts to see light through research and experimentation.
光の観察の歴史。光はすべてに形と色を与えるが、われわれは光そのものを見ることができない。人類は研究を重ね、光を見ようと試みてきた。

Mock-up test　モックアップ実験

"Time of light" was measured using water. Water particles became points of light at the light emission time of 5/1,000,000 second.
光を水に照射し、光の時間の観測を試みた。100万分の5秒の発光時間により、光は点となり水滴の中で輝き始めた。

LIGHT is TIME

LIGHT is TIME | Milan, Italy 2014 | installation completed

Light is time and time is light.
If there is no light, there is no time. Time started in our minds when we became aware of the slow movement of the sun from left to right and the consequent arrival of darkness— perhaps when we started moving around on our two feet. We started measuring time when Ancient Mesopotamians started measuring the length of the shadow in relation to the movement of the sun. Ancient Egyptians observed the movement of the sun multiple times and discovered "time periods", which led them to divide time and develop a solar calendar. Later, humans discovered outer space when the notion of the universe shifted from geocentrism to heliocentrism and we started measuring the distance between the earth and the planets or stars based on the light-year. Thus, light became an indicator of time, and time became light.
In our installation "LIGHT is TIME", light and time are inseparable. The space is filled with infinite numbers of sparkling watch base plates and the light constantly keeps moving. Light, along with sounds, fill the space and the space, enhanced by light and sounds, becomes a memory.

光は時間であり時間は光である。もし光がなければ時間が生まれることはなかった。遠い昔、人類が二足歩行を始めた頃、地平から昇った太陽が天高く昇り、遠い地平に向かって再び沈み、気がつくと闇が訪れることを認識したとき、われわれ人類のなかで時間の観念が始まったのかもしれない。メソポタミア文明は太陽の光によって影が伸びる長さを測り、人類は「時間の計測」を始めた。エジプト文明は太陽を中心に文明を発達させ、その動きを何度も観測し「周期の発見」をしたことで時間は分割され太陽暦が生まれる。そして天動説から地動説へと移ろい、天体の存在に気づき、宇宙という空間を発見し、惑星や銀河系の観測を行って距離を光年で計測した。そして光は光速となり、光は時間として時間は光となって示されることになった。そこで、分かつことのできない光と時間をインスタレーションで表現した。無数に輝く時計の基盤装置によって空間が埋め尽くされ、絶え間なく光が動き続ける。光は音とともに空間を満たし、空間は音と光によって記憶へと昇華される。

Copernicus Planisphere from *Harmonia Macrocosmica* 『大宇宙の調和』よりコペルニクス星座早見盤 (1660)

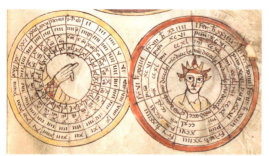
Division of days and weeks 日と週の分割図 (9C)

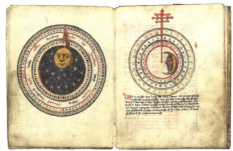
Sun and moon calendar 太陰太陽暦 (1496)

Ptolemaic Universe chart プトレマイオス天体図 (1568)

Cosmographicus Liber by Petrus Apianus
『コスモグラフィア』ペトルス・アピアヌス (1524)

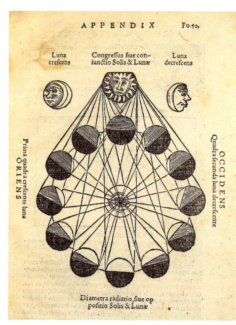
Chart showing the position of the Moon 月の位置表 (1551)

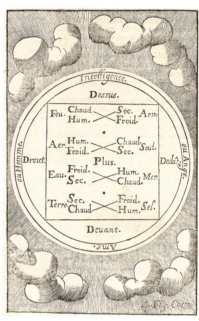
Alchemical processes 錬金術解説 (1657)

The planisphere of Brahe ブラーエの天動説 (1660)

Scenography of the planetary orbits 惑星の軌道 (1660)

The sun in an eccentric orbit 太陽の偏心軌道 (1660)

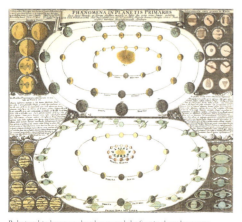
Relationship between the planets and the Sun in the solar system
惑星と太陽の関係性 (1730)

Synopsis of the universe
宇宙の概要図 (1742)

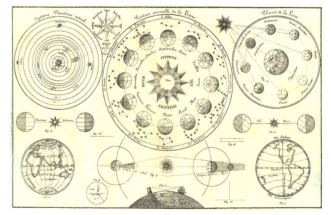
Diagram showing the positional relationship between the Earth and the Sun
地球と太陽の位置関係を示した図 (1834)

Time started when light started. Everything started from light, and light became time. Time is light, and light is time.
光の始まりは時間の始まりである。すべては光から始まり、光は時間となった。時間は光であり、光は時間である。

Concept model　コンセプト模型

The light installation is an installation of time. We created a space where people are immersed in light and sense of time.
光のインスタレーションは時間のインスタレーションである。光に包まれることで、時間を想起させる空間をつくりたいと思った。

time is TIME

time is TIME | Milan, Italy 2016 | installation completed

"What is time?" We wanted to further explore this simple question about time. Standing on earth, we feel that time is constantly moving, but in fact, it is the earth that is constantly moving. The earth rotates on its axis at a speed of 465m per second and rotates around the sun at a speed of 30km per second. All things are constantly moving while being pulled down to the ground by gravity. When something is born into this world, something disappears from this world. When something is about to start somewhere, something is about to end elsewhere. People in the world refer to this finite phenomenon on earth, where everything keeps moving, as "time." On the other hand, time in the universe is absolute. The universe is comprised of matter and energy and there is no beginning and end of time. The universe is driven solely by the forces of matter and energy. Time in the universe is based on the absolute system referred to as "TIME". We interpreted "time" as an organism on the finite earth and "TIME" as an infinite system in the universe. We juxtaposed the two aspects of time in this spatial installation, "time is TIME."

「時間とは何か?」この最も単純な時間への問い掛けをより深く探求したいと思った。地球では時間はいつも動いているように感じる。しかし、時間が動いているのではない、地球が動いているのである。地球は1秒間に465mの距離を自転し、同じ1秒間に30kmの速さで太陽の周りを移動している。すべてが動いていて、すべてが重力によって支えられ、世界のどこかで何かが生まれれば、世界のどこかで何かが消え、いま何かが始まろうとするとき、いまどこかで何かが終わろうとする。世界のそうしたすべてが動き続ける有限の地球の時間を「time」と呼んだ。その一方で、宇宙の時間は絶対である。宇宙ではすべてが物質とエネルギーによって成り立ち、宇宙には時間の始まりも時間の終わりも存在しない。宇宙は物質とエネルギーの力によって動かされ、その厳格なシステムによる宇宙の時間を「TIME」と呼んだ。「time」は有限な地球の中にある時間として、「TIME」は有限ではない宇宙のシステマティックな時間として、このふたつの時間を並置したひとつのインスタレーション「time is TIME」が生まれた。

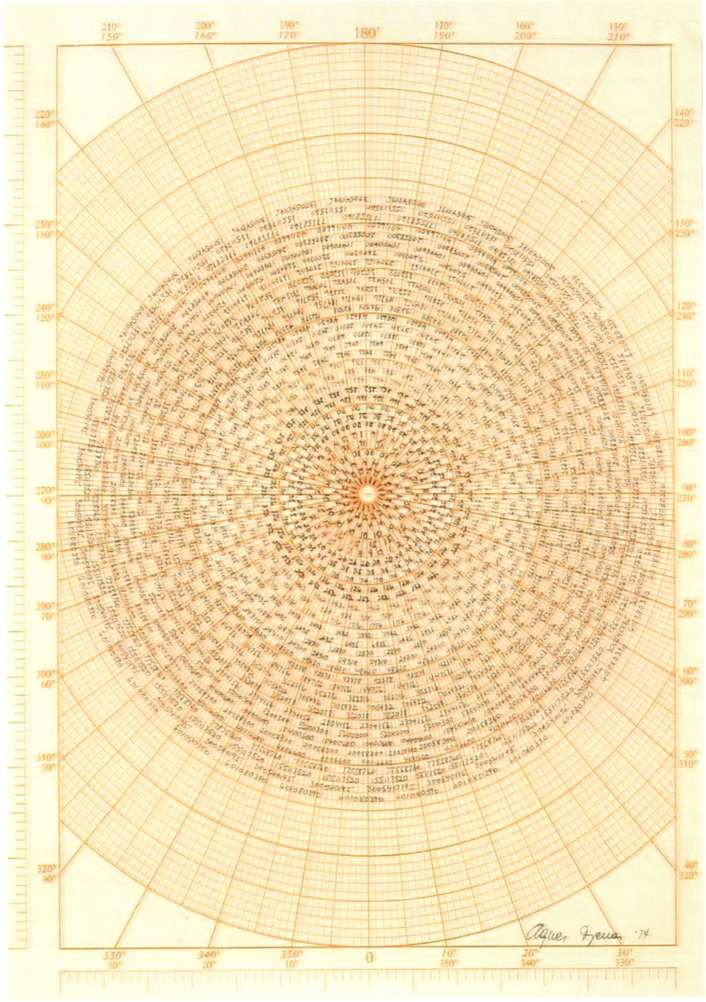

Sun mathematics by Agnes Denes 「サンマスマティクス」アグネス・デネス (1974)

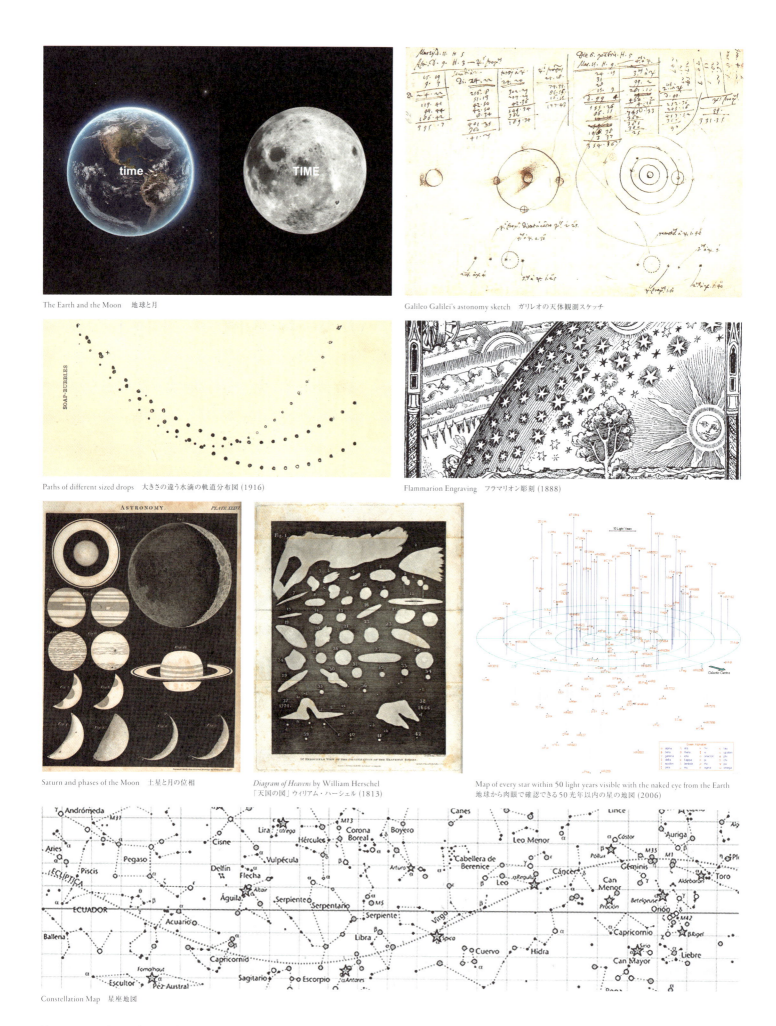

The Earth and the Moon　地球と月

Galileo Galilei's astonomy sketch　ガリレオの天体観測スケッチ

Paths of different sized drops　大きさの違う水滴の軌道分布図 (1916)

Flammarion Engraving　フラマリオン彫刻 (1888)

Saturn and phases of the Moon　土星と月の位相

Diagram of Heavens by William Herschel
「天国の図」ウィリアム・ハーシェル (1813)

Map of every star within 50 light years visible with the naked eye from the Earth
地球から肉眼で確認できる50光年以内の星の地図 (2006)

Constellation Map　星座地図

Time on earth is a finite phenomenon in cycles of birth and death. Time in the universe is absolute and infinite.
地球は周期的な時間があり生命は生まれては消えていく有限の時間。しかし宇宙では物質は空間によって相対化され、時間は絶対であり有限ではない。

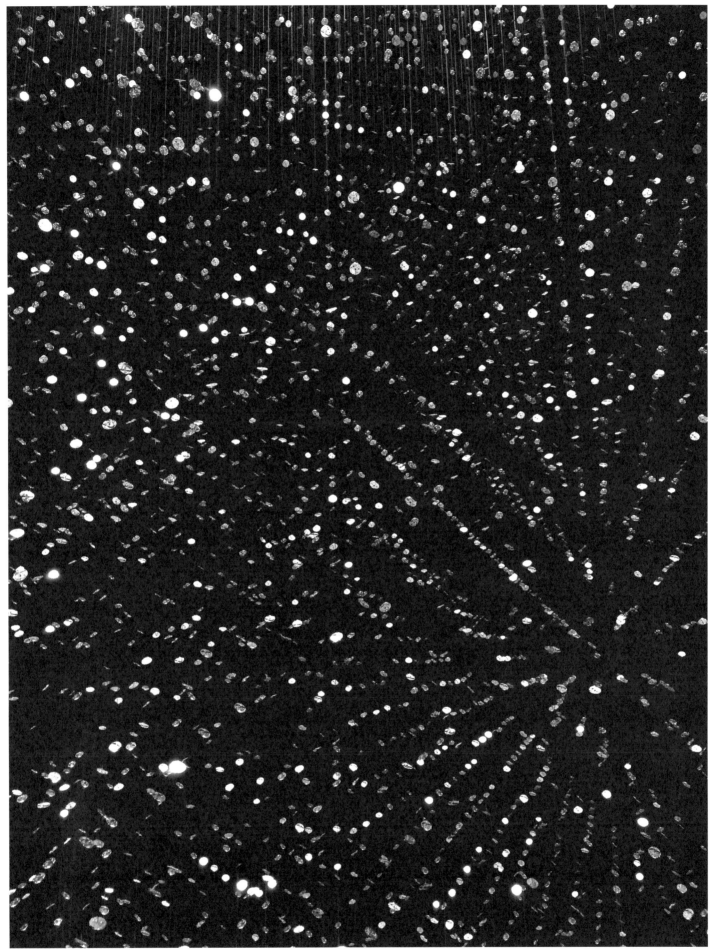

Mock-up test　モックアップ実験

The universe is comprised of substance and energy. There is no past or future. Time in the universe may be a notion of infinity.
宇宙は物質とエネルギーで満たされている。そこには時間の過去も未来もない。時間は観念であり、それは無限なのかもしれない。

Images

Estonian National Museum

エストニア国立博物館

114

Kofun Stadium - New National Stadium Japan

新国立競技場案　古墳スタジアム

146

10 kyoto

10 kyoto

152

Wonderground -
Natural History Museum of Denmark

Wonderground - デンマーク自然科学博物館

158

Arthur Rimbaud Museum

アルチュール・ランボー美術館

164

Hirosaki Contemporary Art Museum

（仮称）弘前市芸術文化施設

170

Shibuya Department Store

渋谷デパートメントストア

178

Twin Towers in Kai Tak Development

カイタック・ツインタワー

184

Yokohama Station Department Store

（仮称）横浜駅デパートメントストア

190

Chiso Building

千總本社ビル

196

A House for Oiso

A House for Oiso

202

Todoroki House in Valley

Todoroki House in Valley

214

Weekend House in Fontainebleau

フォンテーヌブロー週末住宅

228

Toraya Paris

とらやパリ店

234

Luce Tempo Luogo

Luce Tempo Luogo

242

LIGHT is TIME

LIGHT is TIME

250

time is TIME

time is TIME

256

Estonian National Museum

エストニア国立博物館 | Tartu, Estonia 2006-16

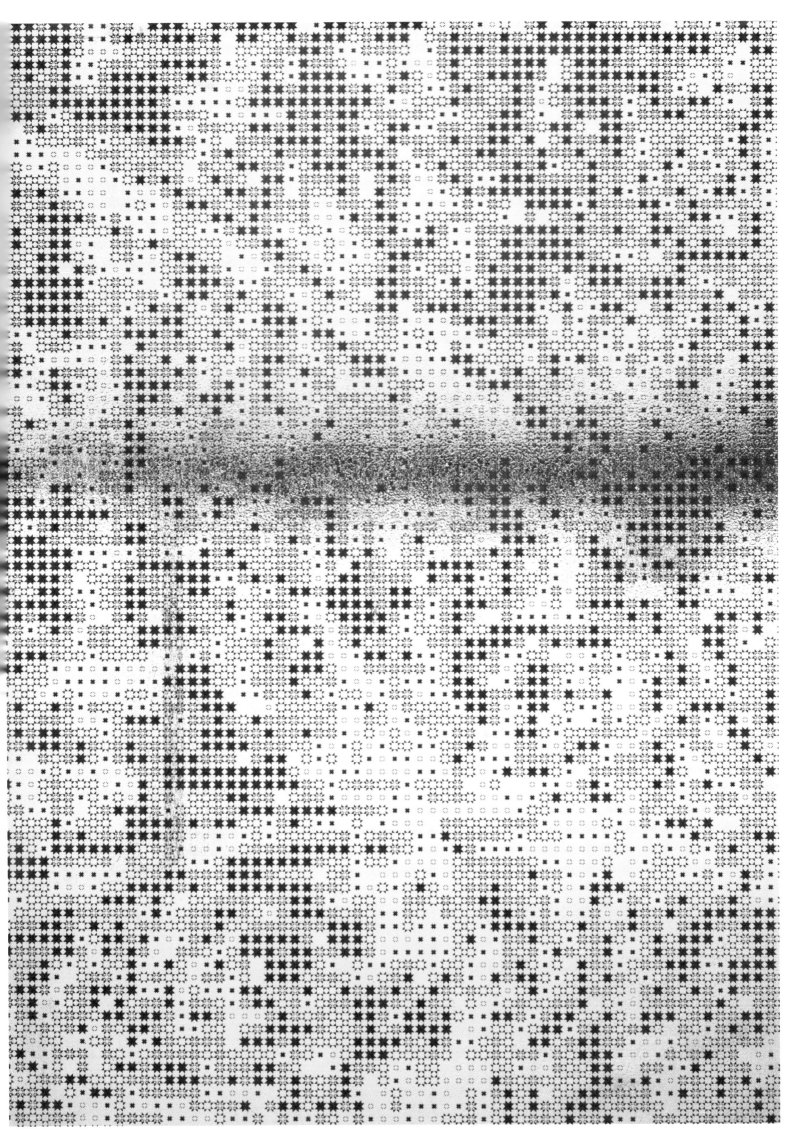

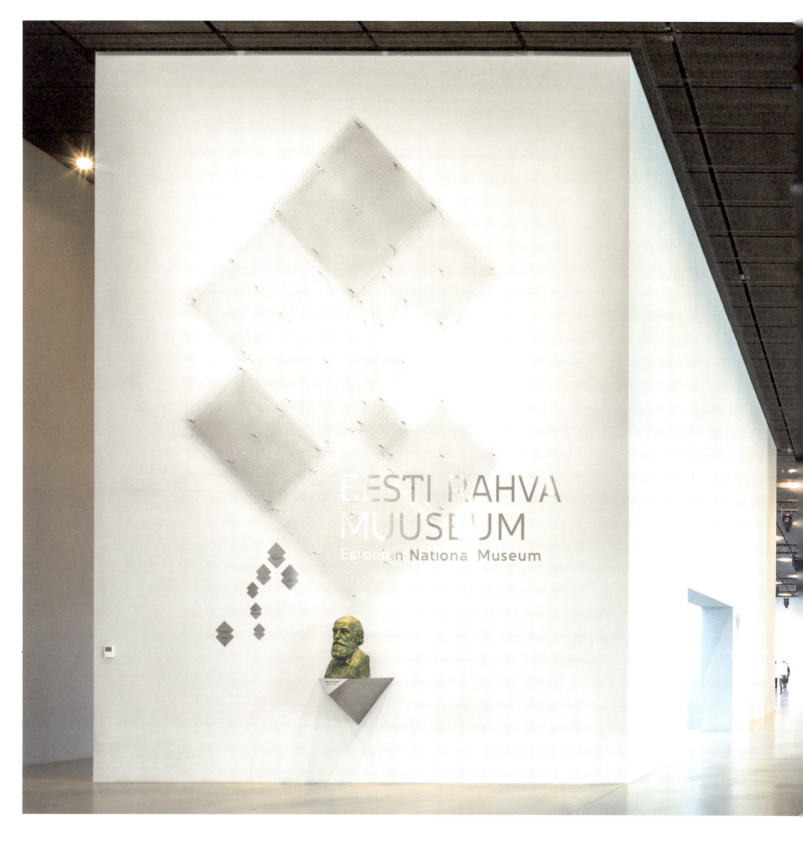

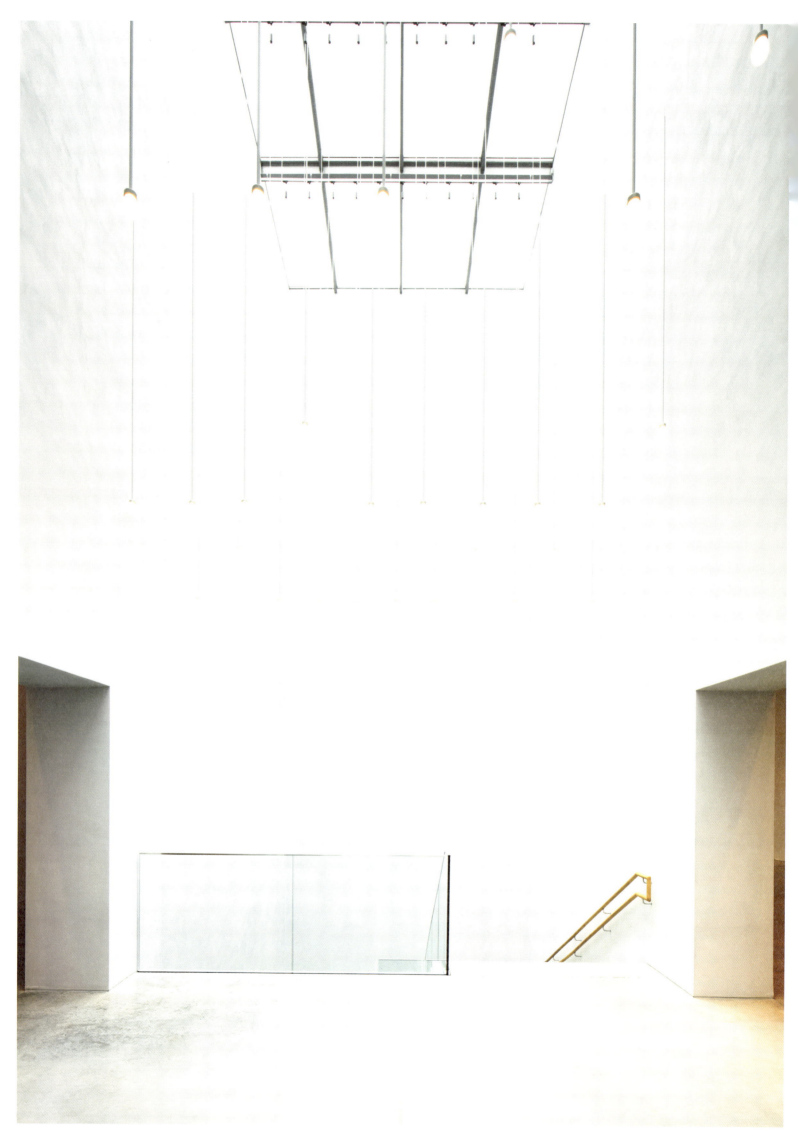

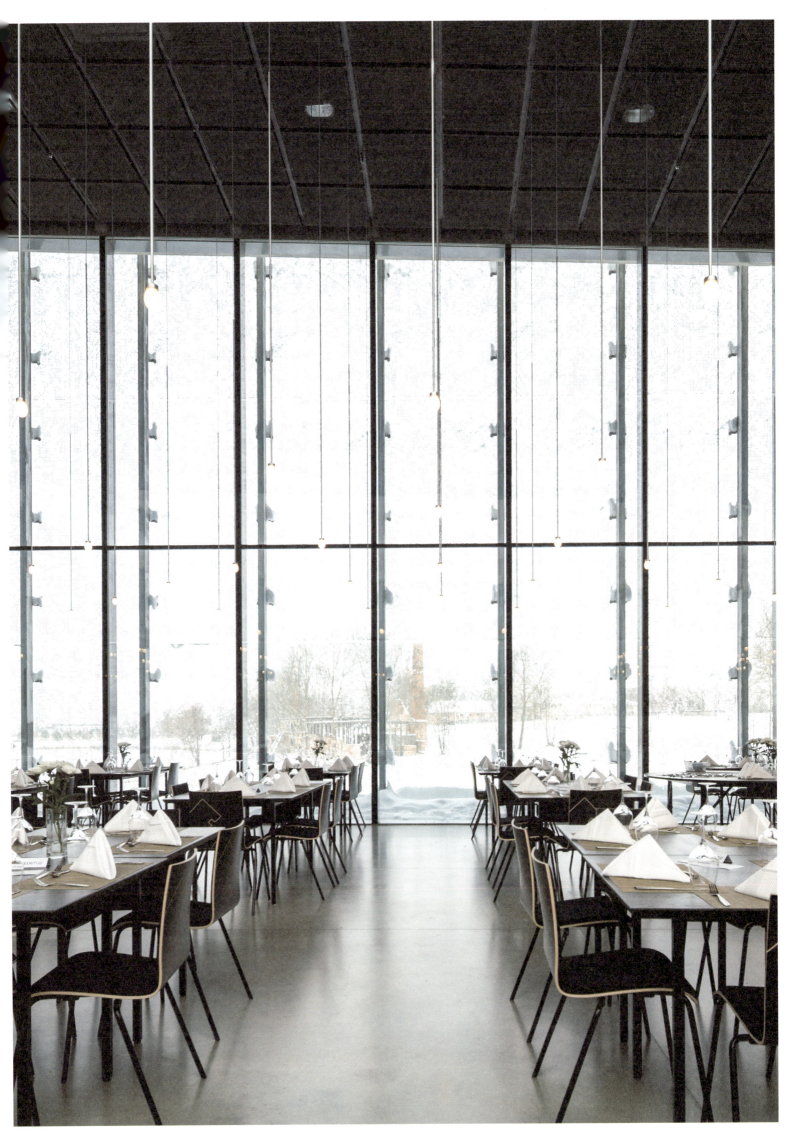

10 kyoto

10 kyoto | Kyoto, Japan 2017-

Wonderground - Natural History Museum of Denmark

Wonderground - デンマーク自然科学博物館 | Copenhagen, Denmark 2009

Arthur Rimbaud Museum

アルチュール・ランボー美術館　|　Charleville-Mézières, France　2012

Hirosaki Contemporary Art Museum

（仮称）弘前市芸術文化施設 | Hirosaki, Japan 2017-

Shibuya Department Store

渋谷デパートメントストア | Tokyo, Japan 2015

Twin Towers in Kai Tak Development

カイタック・ツインタワー | Hong Kong, China 2017

Yokohama Station Department Store

（仮称）横浜駅デパートメントストア ｜ Yokohama, Japan 2016-

Chiso Building

千總本社ビル | Kyoto, Japan 2017-

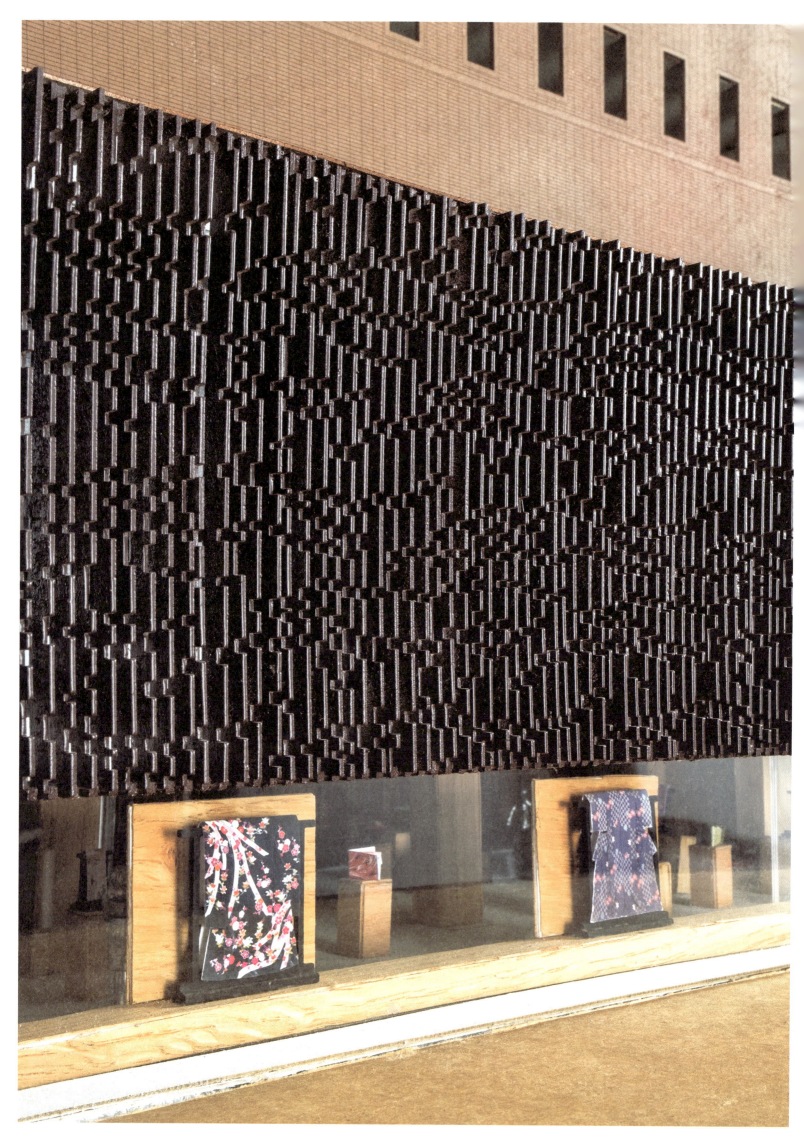

A House for Oiso

A House for Oiso | Kanagawa, Japan 2014-15

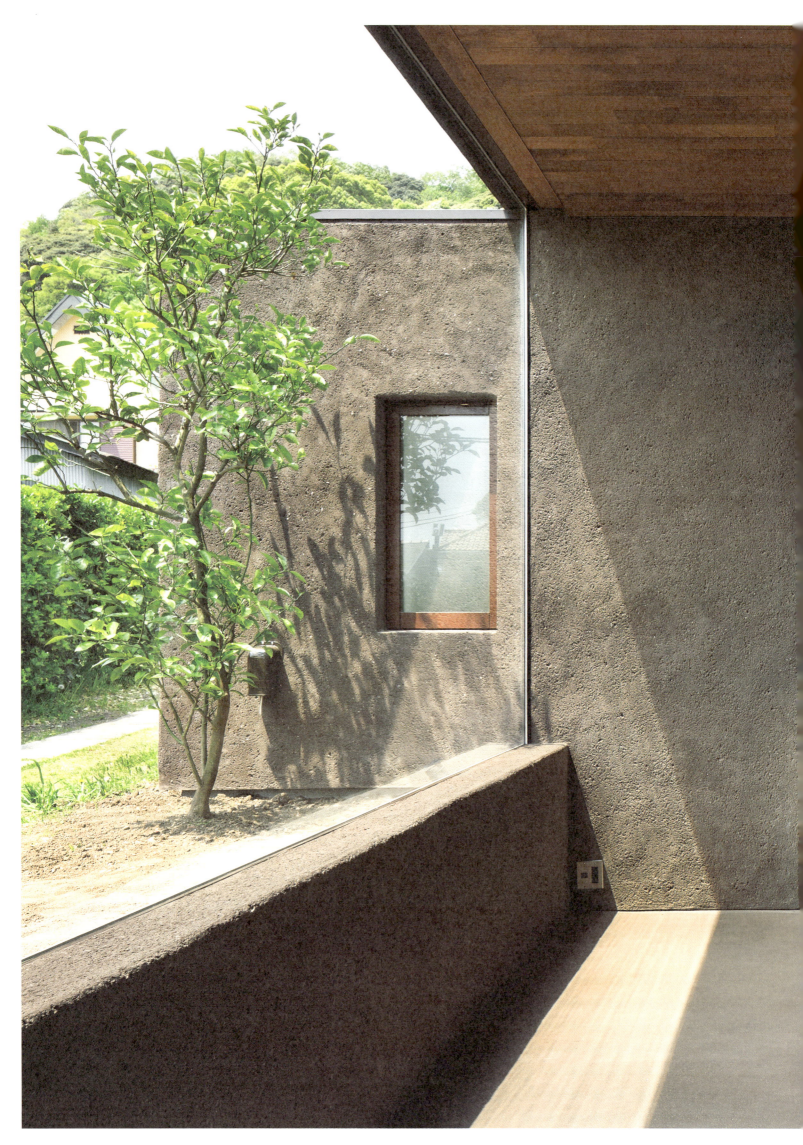

Todoroki House in Valley

Todoroki House in Valley | Tokyo, Japan 2017-18

Weekend House in Fontainebleau

フォンテーヌブロー週末住宅 │ Fontainebleau, France 2017-

Toraya Paris

とらやパリ店 | Paris, France 2015

Luce Tempo Luogo

Luce Tempo Luogo | Milan, Italy 2011

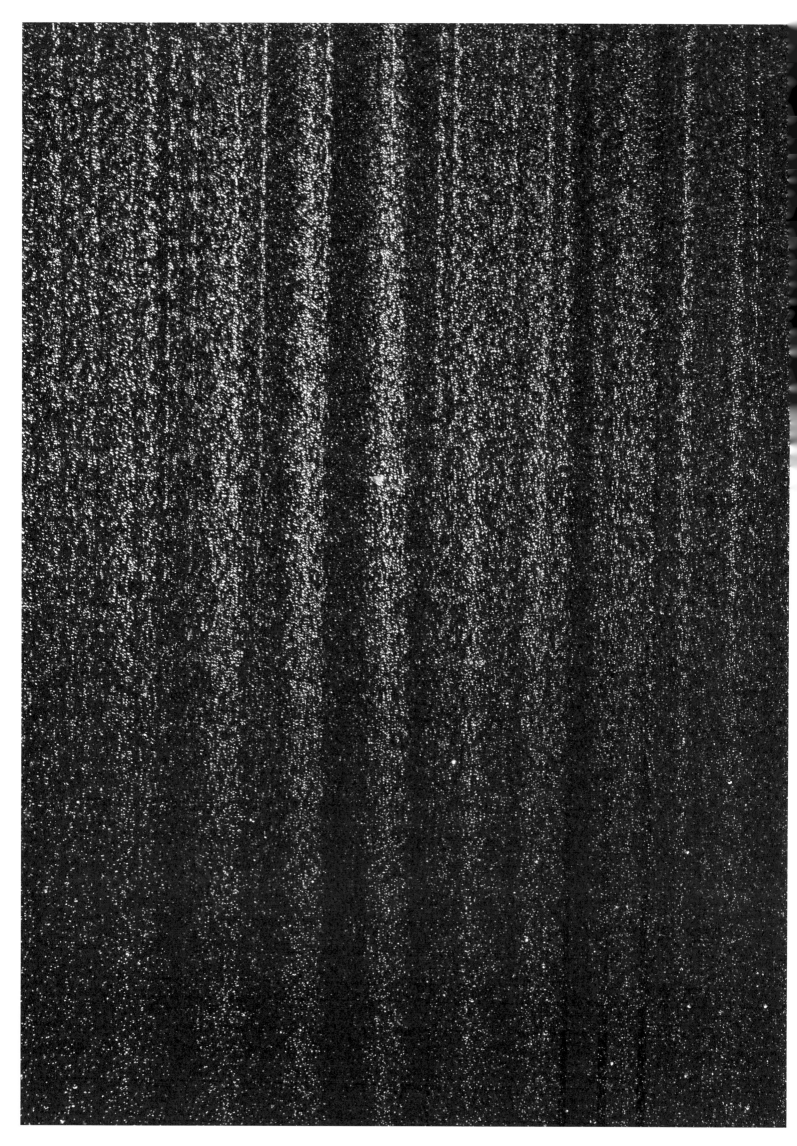

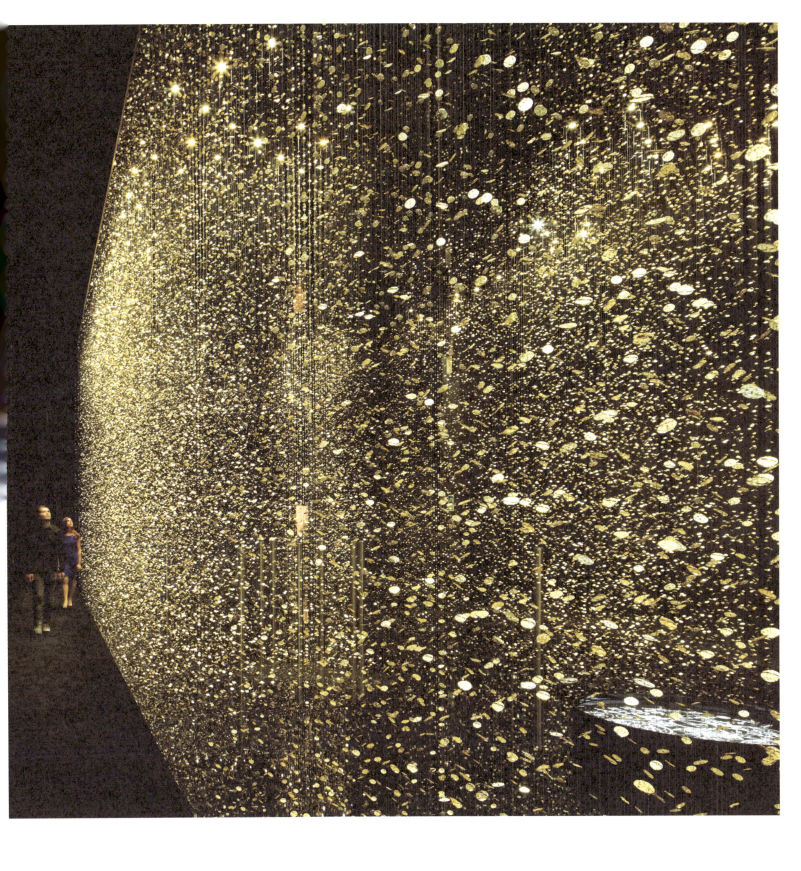

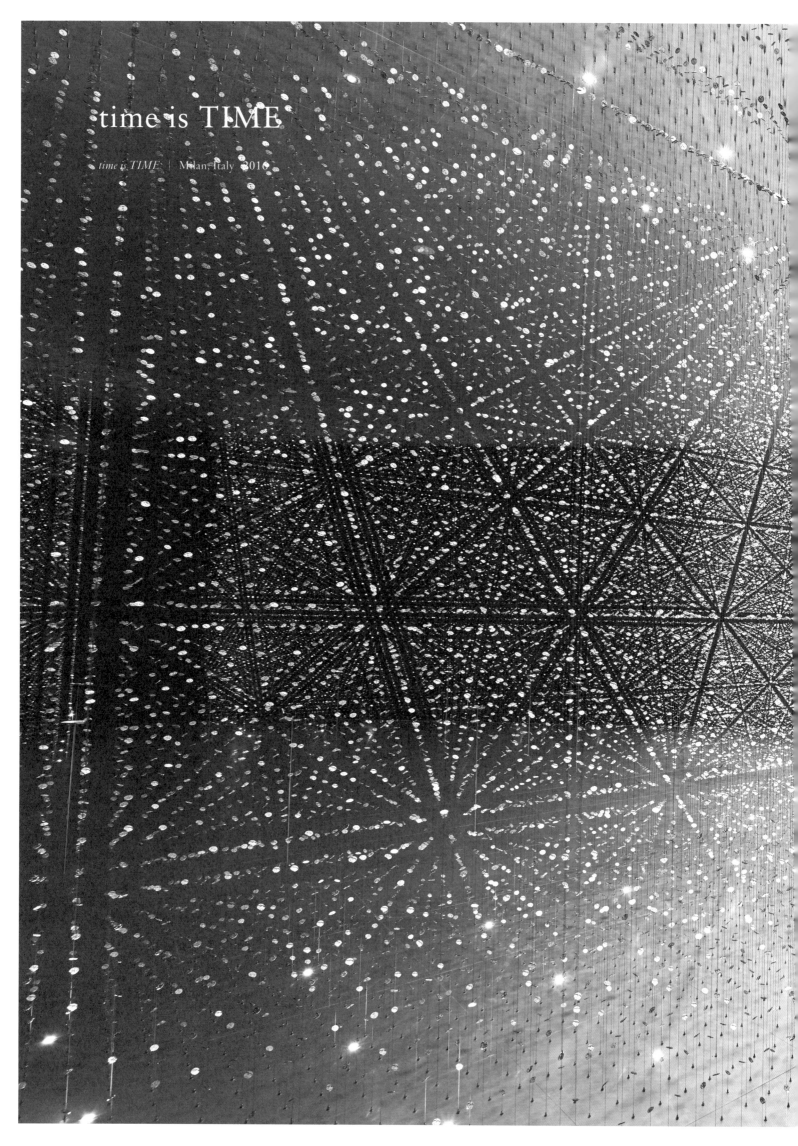

time is TIME

time is TIME | Milan, Italy 2016

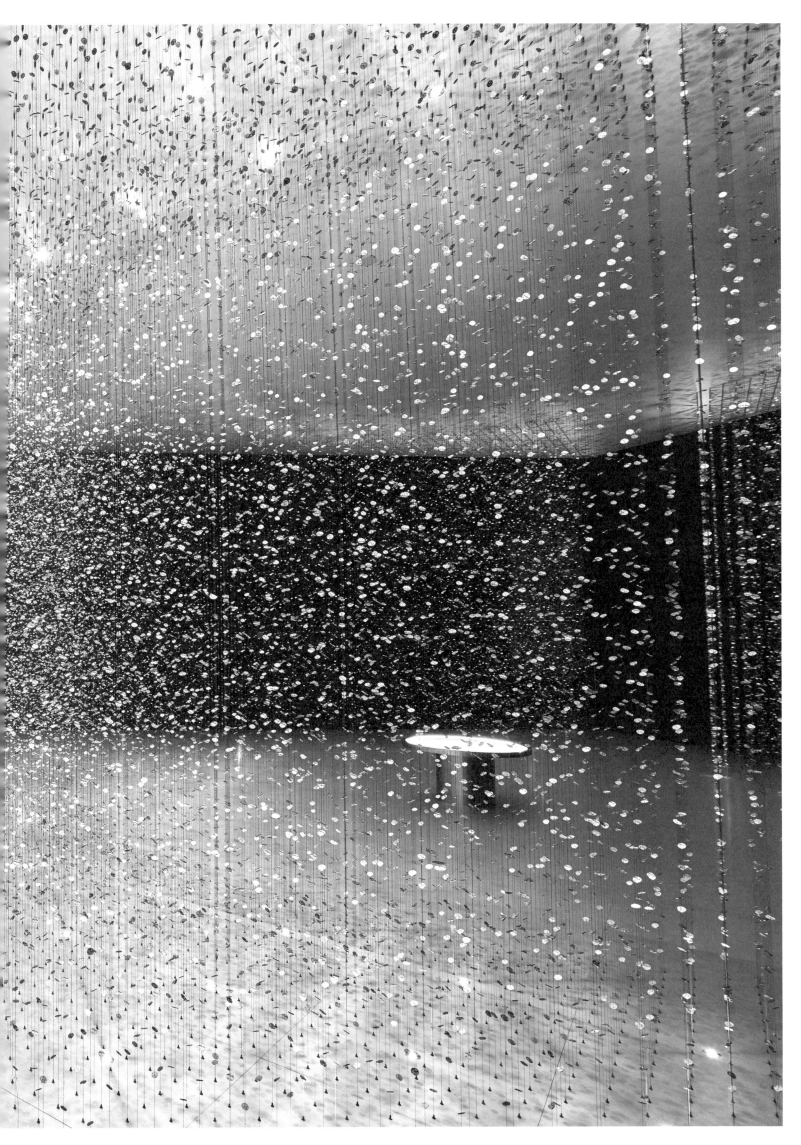

Drawings

Estonian National Museum

エストニア国立博物館

264

Kofun Stadium - New National Stadium Japan

新国立競技場案　古墳スタジアム

270

10 kyoto

10 kyoto

274

Wonderground -
Natural History Museum of Denmark

Wonderground - デンマーク自然科学博物館

278

Arthur Rimbaud Museum

アルチュール・ランボー美術館

280

Hirosaki Contemporary Art Museum

（仮称）弘前市芸術文化施設

282

Shibuya Department Store

渋谷デパートメントストア

286

Twin Towers in Kai Tak Development

カイタック・ツインタワー

288

Yokohama Station Department Store

（仮称）横浜駅デパートメントストア

290

Chiso Building

千總本社ビル

294

A House for Oiso

A House for Oiso

296

Todoroki House in Valley

Todoroki House in Valley

298

Weekend House in Fontainebleau

フォンテーヌブロー週末住宅

300

Toraya Paris

とらやパリ店

302

Luce Tempo Luogo

Luce Tempo Luogo

303

LIGHT is TIME

LIGHT is TIME

304

time is TIME

time is TIME

305

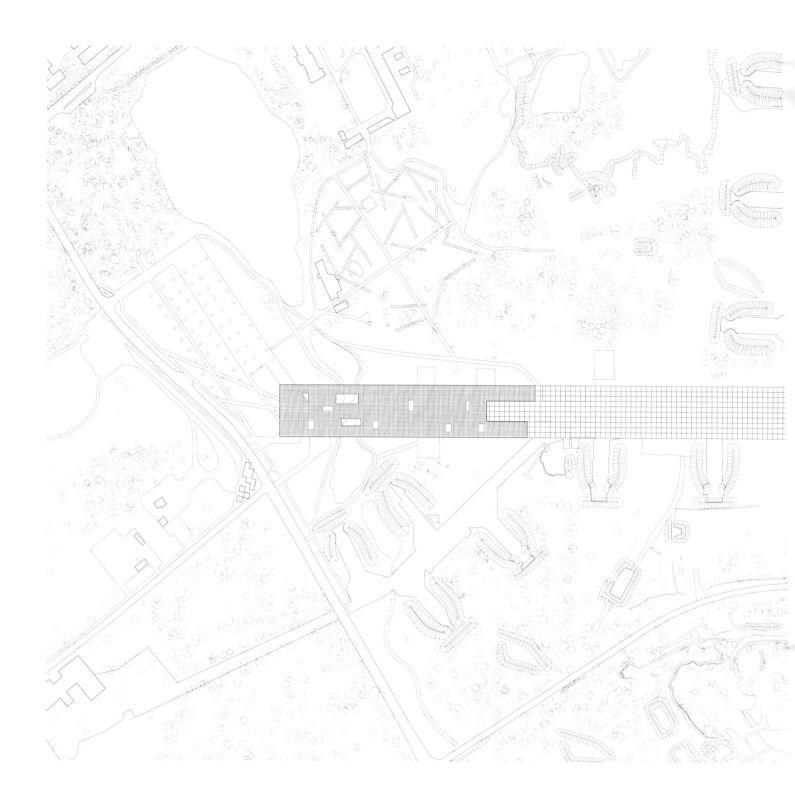

Estonian National Museum

エストニア国立博物館 | Tartu, Estonia 2006-16

The Estonia National Museum has a collection based on the history of Estonia and its people since the Ice Age. The building, 72m wide and 335m long, connects to the former Soviet airbase runway with a total length of 1.5km. A large beam weighing 200 tons carries the entrance canopy 14m in height and 42m in depth. It is supported by a post-tensioning method, and the middle section of the building spans 42m over the lake. The glass skin protects the building from the extreme winter weather conditions while blending it into the landscape. On the glass, we used the symbol of the Octagram, representing hope for the future, to compose collages depicting the snow and forest landscapes of Estonia. The building contains public spaces, exhibition rooms, a theater, a library, a restaurant, offices, and storage. People are invited to actively use public spaces and explore the entire museum. Various events including music and dance performances, movie festivals, and conferences are regularly held at the museum. In 2018, the museum hosted the 100th Anniversary Ceremony of the Republic of Estonia and a new chapter in Estonian history was started from here.

siteplan 1/5000

エストニア国立博物館は、エストニアの氷河期から現在までの民族の歴史を収蔵する施設である。幅72m、長さ355mの建物が後方の滑走路跡へとつながり、全長1.5kmの建築となる。外観のガラス面は「希望」を示す民族の伝統的なシンボル「Octagram」を用いて、エストニアの森と雪の風景をコラージュした10種類のパターンで構成した。このガラス面は寒冷地の風雨や氷雪による建物の劣化を防ぎ、周辺の森や雪の風景に溶け込んでいく。エントランスの大庇は高さ14m、奥行き42mが約200tの大梁はポストテンションによって支持されており、建物の中央部では42mの大スパンで空中を横切るように湖の上に浮かんでいる。建物内部にはパブリックスペース、展示室、小劇場、図書室、レストラン、オフィス、収蔵庫などがあり、パブリック・スペースを中心に博物館全体が活発に使われるよう計画した。音楽やダンス、映画祭やコンファレンスなどさまざまなイベントが常に催されている。また2018年のエストニア建国100周年の記念式典も、このエストニア国立博物館で催され、ここからまた歴史の第一歩を歩み始めた。

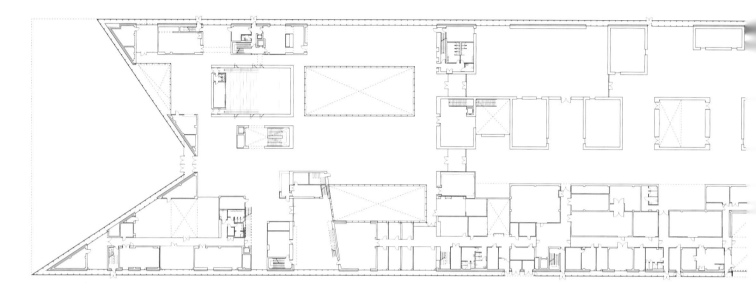

ground floor plan

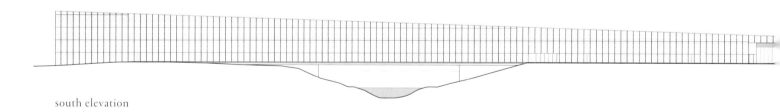

south elevation

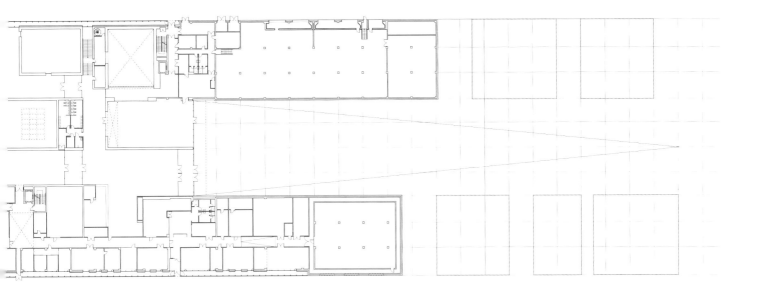

1/1000

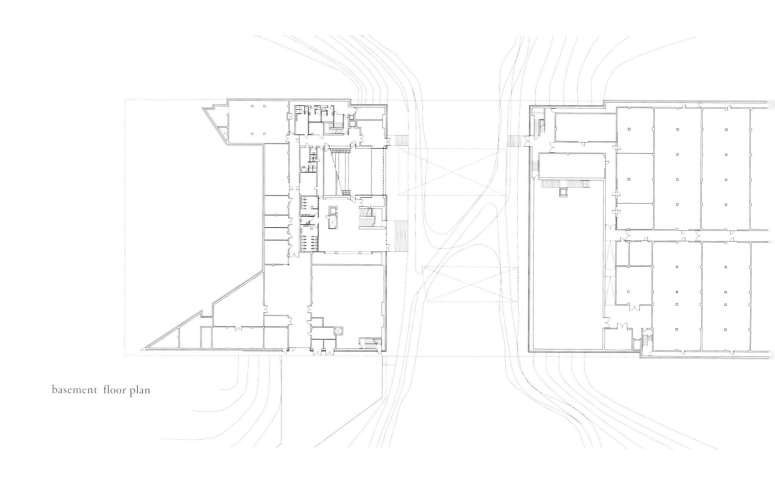

basement floor plan

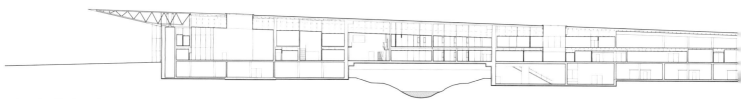

longitudinal section

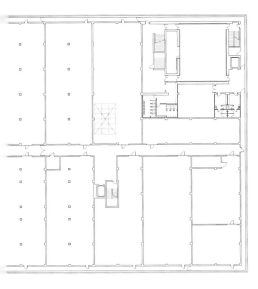

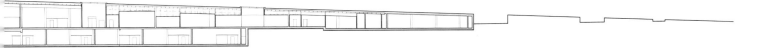

1/1000

siteplan 1/7500

Kofun Stadium - New National Stadium Japan

新国立競技場案 古墳スタジアム | Tokyo, Japan 2012

The international design competition for the New National Stadium Japan, the main stadium for the Tokyo 2020 Olympics/Paralympics, took place in 2012. Stringent design conditions were given including that it be an "all-weather, multi-purpose next-generation stadium accommodating 80,000 spectators" and that there were the necessary disaster prevention measures. The resulting volume of the stadium would inevitably be too large and out of scale with its surroundings in Jingu Gaien. "Kofun Stadium" is a plan to develop a forest for the future corresponding with the Meiji Shrine forest, inspired from kofun, an ancient tumulus in Japan. This forest development will be implemented as a national project: trees gathered from all over Japan will be planted by citizens to connect the memory of the place to the future. Rainwater will be collected and redistributed to the forest, which will help create macroclimates to cool the city. The stadium creates a micro-sustainable ecosystem where damaged patches of grass on the field will be replanted on the roof soil and excess energy accumulated during non-operating time will be supplied to surrounding districts.

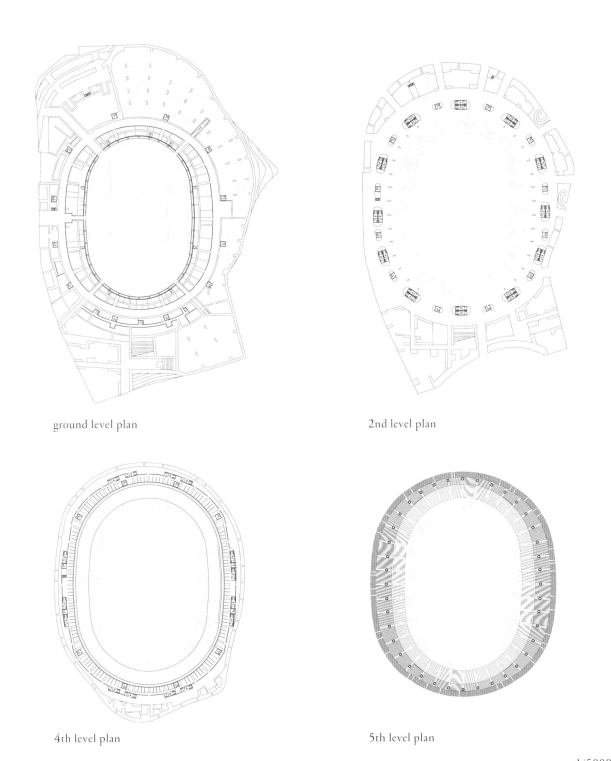

ground level plan

2nd level plan

4th level plan

5th level plan

1/5000

2020年の東京オリンピック・パラリンピックのメインスタジアム計画として、2012年夏に新国立競技場の国際設計競技が開かれた。全天候型の次世代スタジアムとして複数の用途に対応する80,000人収容のスタジアムという与条件を満たし、さらに都心部での避難や防災計画も満たすには、この限られた敷地面積ではスタジアムのボリュームは肥大化し、日本最初の風致地区である神宮外苑の周辺地域とは明らかに異質なスケールとなってしまう。そこで提案した「古墳スタジアム」は、明治神宮の杜と呼応する未来の森をつくる計画であった。森を育てるために雨水を集め細かい霧として散水し、都市の冷却効果としてマクロな環境を形成する。また芝生の破損は屋根面の土へと還元されたり、スタジアムが使われていない間の余分なエネルギーは周辺地区に供給するなど、自然と人工環境の未来を目指す次世代型のスタジアムとした。

west elevation

north elevation

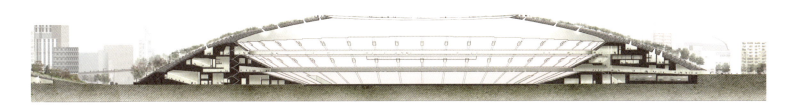

longitudinal section

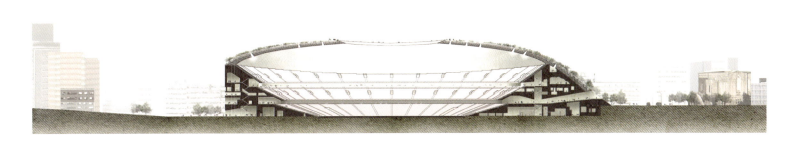

transversal section

1/3500

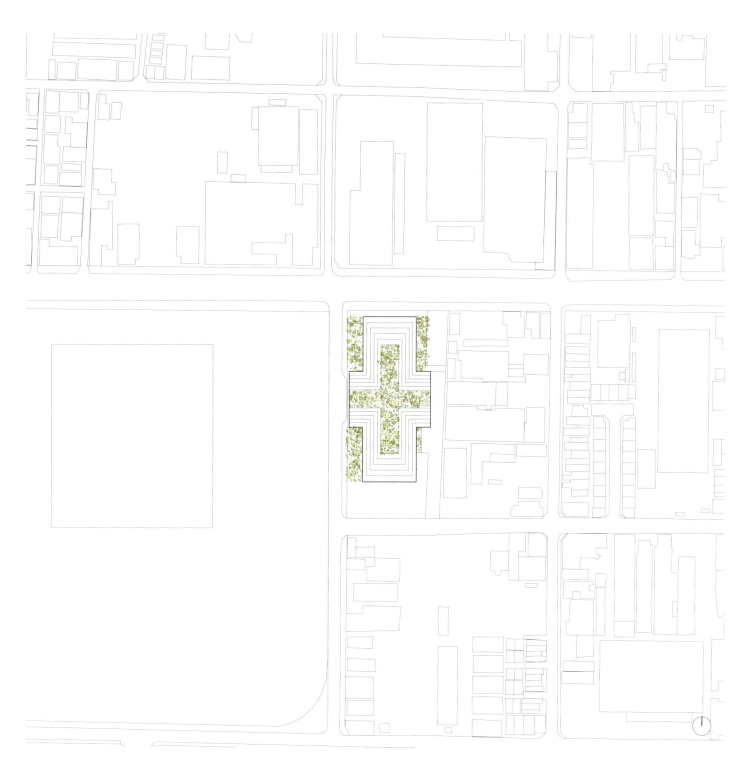

siteplan 1/2000

10 kyoto

10 kyoto | Kyoto, Japan 2017-

We are planning a cultural complex comprising of an art, living, food spaces, and recycling system in Jujo, Kyoto. The first floor is a public food court open to the community where one can enjoy the food cultures of Kyoto and the rest of the world; the second to fifth floors accommodate a new concept living space; the top floor is a contemporary art space, and the rooftop is a sky botanical garden with a panorama view of the city, which we present as a new addition to enhance Kyoto's rich garden culture. The demolition of existing buildings in Kyoto produces an average of 10 tons of waste from wood frame construction components per day. These materials will be recycled into laminated wood and used to clad the building, as part of our project to "collect Kyoto's past to create Kyoto's future." The cross-shaped building on the city grid is clad with wooden walls and sporadically located atrium spaces clustered around the central core to serve as public spaces. Groundwater is fed into the radiant heat system to maintain a constant temperature of 15-17°C and the environmental control system, utilizing renewable energy, maintains the suitable growing environment for plants.

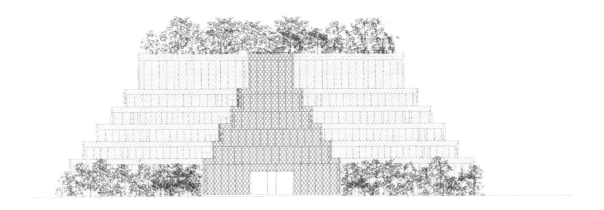

west elevation

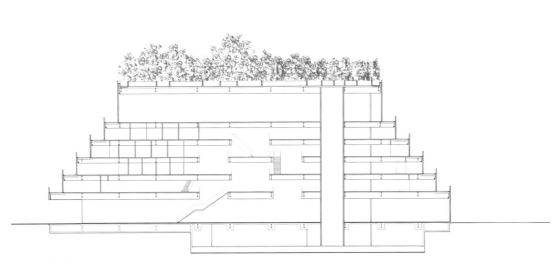

longitudinal section

1/800

京都に新たなアートスペース、リビングスペース、フードスペース、リサイクルシステムが一体となった文化複合施設を計画している。地上1階は地域に開かれた京都と世界の食文化を楽しめるフードスペース、2-5階は新しいコンセプトによるリビングスペース、最上階は現代アートの空間となり、屋上からは京都を見わたしながら京都に新たな空中植物園の風景を加えるものとしている。京都市内で建物の解体によって、1日平均10tほどの木柱・梁・垂木などの軸組部材が廃材となる。それらを集め、接着した「古材集成材」によって建物全体を覆い尽くすことで、「古い京都を集め、新しい京都を創る」プロジェクトとして進行している。象徴的な木製の外壁をもつ東西と南北の軸に十字型の建物は、地下階から最上階まで突き抜けるコアを中心に断続的な吹き抜け空間がパブリックスペースとなる。また地下では地下水を汲み上げることで、年間を通して15-17℃の安定した輻射熱によるミクロな温度調整を行い、再生エネルギーによるシステムで多種多様な植物が育つような環境計画とした。

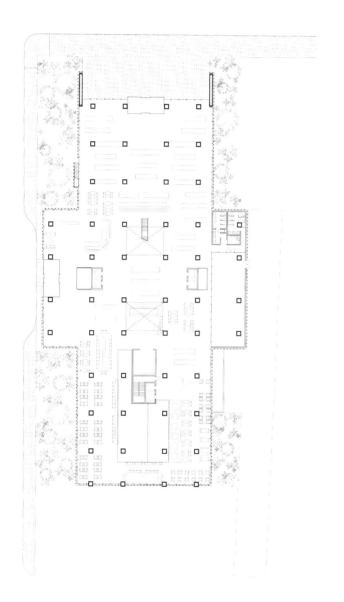

ground floor plan

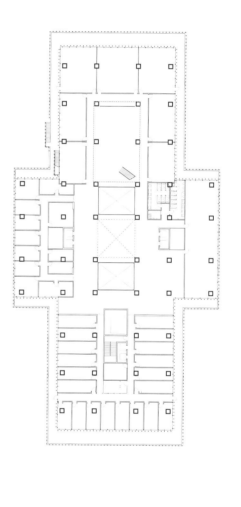

1st floor plan

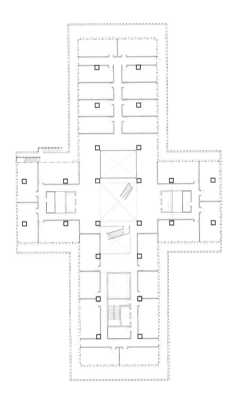
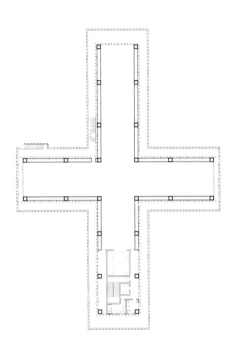

3rd floor plan   5th floor plan   1/800

siteplan 1/2000

Wonderground - Natural History Museum of Denmark

Wonderground - デンマーク自然科学博物館 | Copenhagen, Denmark 2009

The Natural History Museum of Denmark consisted of four separate facilities located at Rosenburg Castle Garden in Copenhagen. In 2009, an international design competition for the museum's expansion plan took place, which aimed to integrate all of the existing facilities into a new exhibition facility. Our proposed scheme consisted of two main facilities connected via an underground space like an excavation site. Visitors enter from a main entrance made by hollowing out a courtyard of an adjacent building. The interior is comprised of interconnected exhibition spaces divided into different themes, with the exhibition sequence unfolding as one goes from one space to another. The volume of each exhibition space is determined according to the scale and content of each theme. Structural concrete cores are dispersed throughout the interior and loosely divide the open space into sub-spaces where people see and can be seen. Some of the enclosed spaces are used as exhibition rooms and others accommodate vertical circulation. The roof features a herb garden cascading down into a courtyard which helps develop a diverse botanical environment.

plan

longitudinal section

1/1250

デンマーク自然科学博物館はコペンハーゲンの中心部にあるオールボー公園内に4棟の施設がばらばらにあった。この博物館のすべての施設を結びつけ、自然科学を体験する展示施設の拡張計画のコンペが2009年に行われた。ローゼンボー城のある公園や市立美術館が隣接する既存の建物の中庭をくり抜いて設けられたメインエントランスが地上からの来場者を迎え入れ、発掘現場のような地層空間によってふたつの主要な施設を地下でつなぐ計画とした。内部では自然科学のテーマによって分類された分野におけるミクロからマクロまでの物質の大小によって展示空間のボリュームを設定し、空間が連結しながら展開していくような構成とした。またコンクリートの構造体のコアによって空間を分散させ、閉じた空間が垂直動線や密閉した展示室として活用され、開かれた空間は分節されながらも、それぞれの空間が見えたり・見られたりする一体空間として開放的につないでいる。また屋根はボタニカルガーデンとしてさまざまなハーブが植えられ、それらの植物が地下へとなだれ込むような中庭も設けられている。さまざまな植生がそれぞれの庭で育成される。

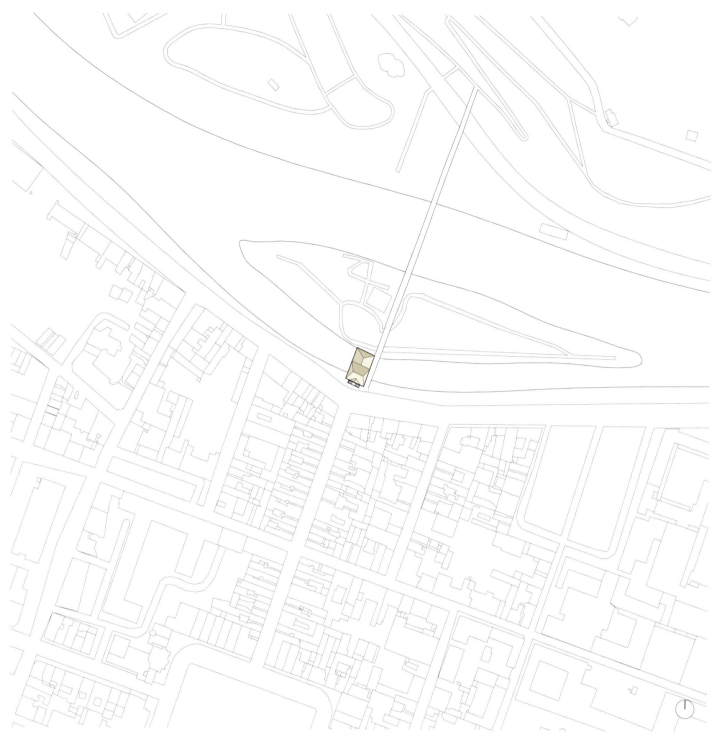

siteplan 1/2000

Arthur Rimbaud Museum

アルチュール・ランボー美術館 | Charleville-Mézières, France 2012

The aim of this project is to renovate a 17th-century water mill built along a uniform streetscape in the center of Charleville-Mézières into a museum dedicated to Arthur Rimbaud. The water mill is a historic landmark of monumental stone masonry and brick walls on the exterior, and in contrast the interior is simply constructed of wood. Our proposal preserves the history of the building by keeping the exterior walls while demolishing all of the inside wooden floors in order to start the museum from an "empty" historic landmark. A glass floor is laid below the central atrium, exposing the view of the river underneath. The visitors' circulation paths and stairs spiral up throughout the atrium, transforming this museum into a theater space. The exhibition space is a "space of reminiscence" between massive walls rather than an "exhibition room", where Rimbaud's few personal effects are displayed like objects left behind in the course of his journey. The intensity and genius of Rimbaud's life and work are powerfully expressed through dramatic architectural manipulation where the interior is regenerated through destruction while the historic building envelope is kept as it is.

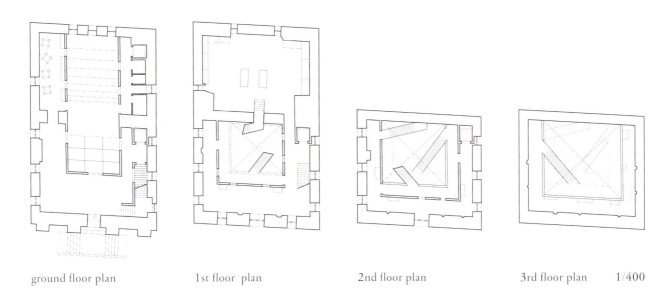

ground floor plan　　　　1st floor plan　　　　2nd floor plan　　　　3rd floor plan　　　1/400

longitudinal section　　　　　　　　　　　　　　　　　　　　　　　　　　　　　　　　1/400

フランス北東部にあるシャルルヴィル・メツィエの中心部にある統一的な街並みの軸線上に建てられた17世紀の水車小屋を改修してアルチュール・ランボーの美術館とする計画であった。歴史的建造物であるこの水車小屋は、モニュメンタルな石造りと煉瓦の堅牢な外壁とは裏腹に、内側の床や壁は簡素な木造であった。そこで建物の歴史性を保存しながらも、すべての床を取り壊し、空っぽの歴史的建造物の状態から美術館をつくることを始めた。まず中央の吹き抜け空間の床面にはガラスが敷かれ、床下に流れる川がむき出しになる。そして上部はボイド空間でありながらも空中では下部から上部に向かって階段状に空間が広がり、来場者の動線によってここは美術館でありながら劇場空間となる。展示空間には数少ないランボーの遺留品が旅路のように置かれ、展示室というよりも外壁の歴史的な分厚い壁の間に挟み込まれたような追憶の空間となる。歴史的建造物を残しながら、その内部を破壊し生きた空間に蘇らせる劇性こそランボーの美術館としてふさわしい建築であると考えた。

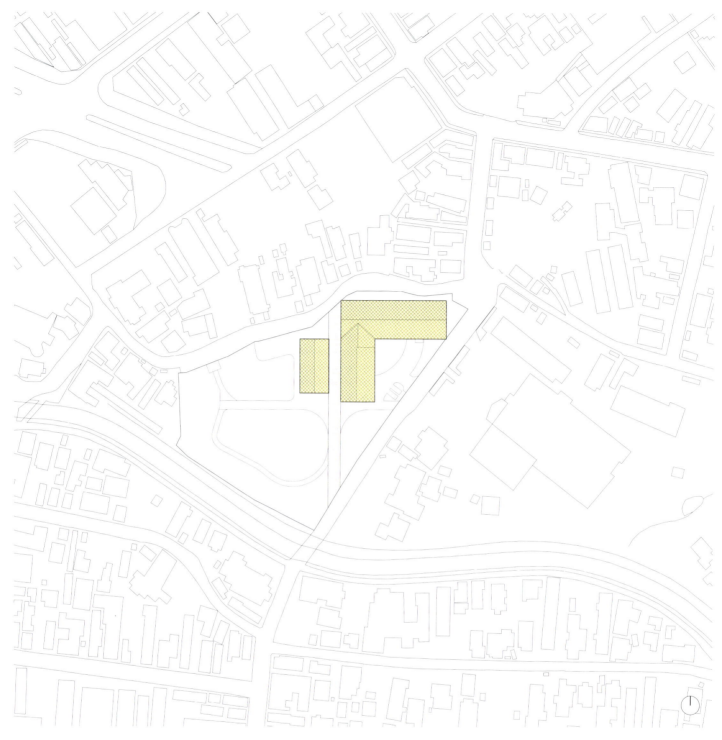

siteplan 1/2000

Hirosaki Contemporary Art Museum

（仮称）弘前市芸術文化施設 | Hirosaki, Japan 2017-

The brick warehouses in Hirosaki will be converted into a contemporary art museum. There are few cases of adaptive reuse of architectural heritage in Japan, and most of the historic buildings are doomed to be demolished. As a way to keep the existing warehouse as it is and make it function as an art museum, we applied an advanced seismic retrofitting technique of drilling 50mm diameter holes through the 9m high brick walls at 1000mm intervals, inserting a pre-stressed concrete steel wire into each hole and fastening it to the top of the foundation. The museum is divided into a public wing and a museum wing, both constructed of bricks. The exhibition space can be used for one, or several exhibitions at the same time and there is a 15m high space designed exclusively for a site-specific artwork. The annex building is reconstructed to accommodate a museum shop and cafe. By replacing the old heavy zinc roof with a cider-gold colored roof, the "roof of light" emerges changing its impression constantly along with changes of light throughout the day.

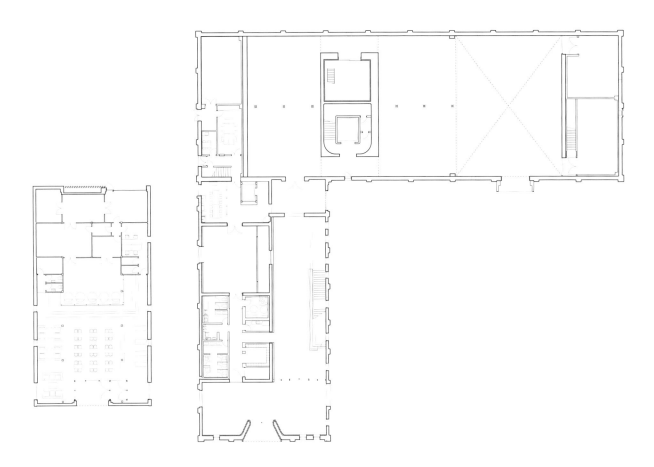

ground floor plan

1/1500

弘前の煉瓦倉庫を美術館にするプロジェクトである。日本では建築文化遺産を現代の文化に積極的に活用するような事例はまだまだ少なく、大半は老朽化か耐震基準を理由に壊されてしまう。そこで美術館のあり方としても煉瓦壁を無傷な状態で残すために、煉瓦壁の高さ9mの上部から1,000mmピッチで直径50mmの穴を開け、そこにPC鋼線を差し込み上部と下部で緊結する、耐震改修の高度な技術を採用した。館内ではパブリック棟とミュージアム棟に分け、改修部分にも改築部分にも煉瓦を用いる空間とした。また展示空間では既存倉庫の質感を活かしながら、個展または複数の展覧会が同時に開催でき、その一部を高さ15mの大空間によるサイトスペシフィックな現代アートと対峙できる空間とした。また解体されるはずであった別棟も再建することで、地域に開かれたミュージアムショップとカフェが運営される。そして老朽化した重い亜鉛の屋根の色をシードルゴールドとすることで、淡い柔らかな朝陽から真赤な夕陽の光へと刻々と表情を変える光の屋根が出現する。

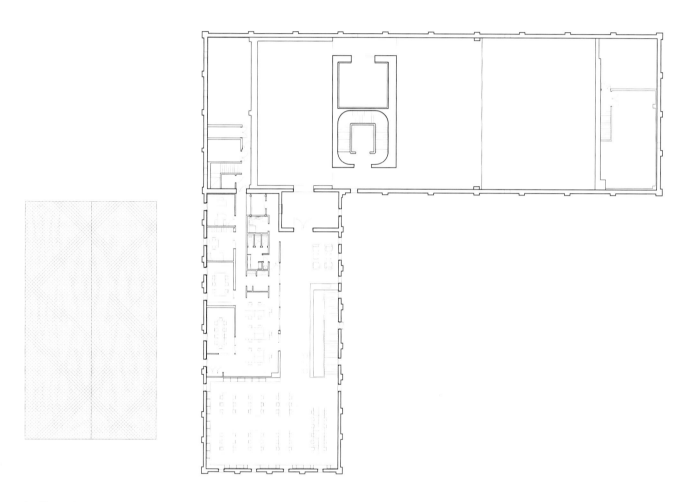

1st floor plan

1/500

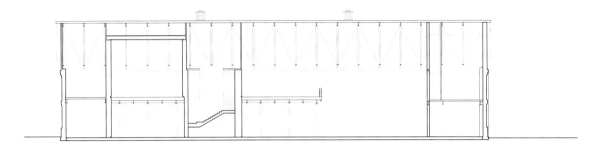

longitudinal section

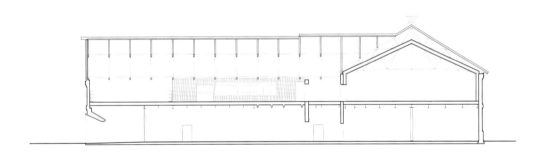

transversal section

south elevation

1/500

siteplan 1/3000

Shibuya Department Store

渋谷デパートメントストア | Tokyo, Japan 2015

We envisioned Shibuya Department Store as architecture that creates the future of Shibuya's street culture. Topographically, Shibuya is located in a valley with many gently sloping streets. Our design intends to directly transform lively interactions on the undulating streets into three-dimensional architectural forms. In general, architects tend to maximize building volumes and ignore the scale of existing streetscapes in commercial developments in the city center. We instead used the scale of small street-level shops as our standard modules and designed a three-dimensional aggregation of these modules organically connected in the same way cells continually proliferate and divide. It is difficult to maintain active customer circulation on the limited site and as a solution to this problem, we placed five cores for vertical circulation and introduced a spatial sequence that unfolds diagonally in section. Our idea was to connect "closed spaces" and "open spaces" diagonally within the spaceband and create a diagonally unfolding shopping space which is neither a classic vertical central atrium style nor stacked horizontal floors based solely on efficient operation.

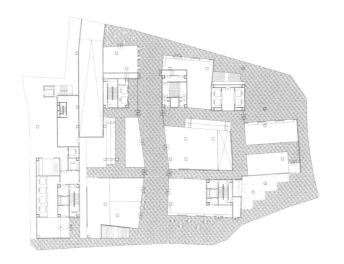
ground floor plan

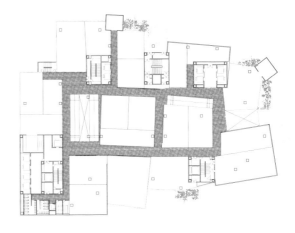
3rd floor plan

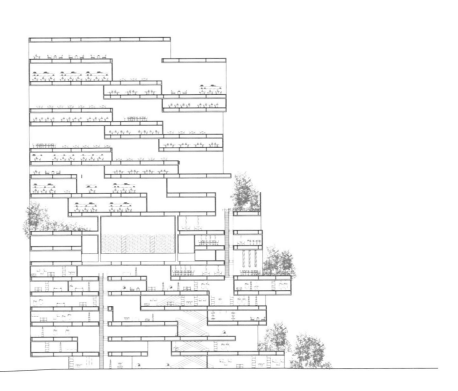
transversal section   1/1200

渋谷デパートメントストアは渋谷のストリートカルチャーの未来を目指すような建築として考えた。渋谷の地形は谷間でもあるため、丘陵地帯のような緩やかな上下移動の多い地域である。その緩やかなストリートの賑わいが途切れずそのまま立体化していくような建築にしたいと考えた。また一方で、都心部の土地開発では、建物のボリュームは最大化され、既存のスケールを無視する計画となりがちである。ここでは小さな路面店サイズを標準として、それらが増殖したり連結しながら細胞分裂するように立体的に集合していることを目指した。また限られた敷地内で回遊性を保つために、等間隔の距離に5つのコアを縦動線として確保する一方、建物の中をより積極的に「斜め」に移動しながら次の空間へと展開する形式を試みた。「ショッピング」という特殊な目的をもつ空間の中で「閉じた空間」と「開いた空間」を斜めにつなぐことで古典的な垂直のセントラルボイドでもなく、効率的に管理されるフロア構成でもない、ダイアゴナルに空間を発見していくプロジェクトとして提案した。

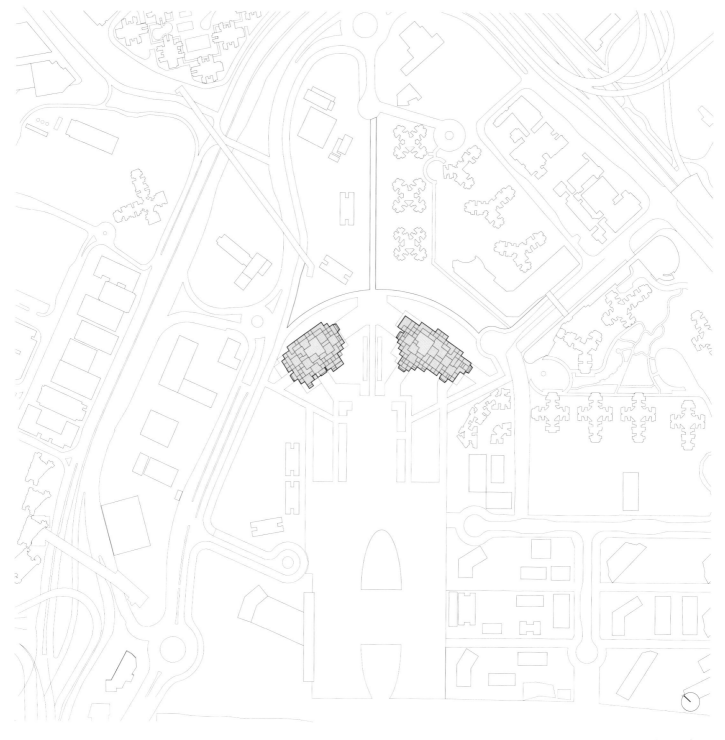

siteplan 1/4000

Twin Towers in Kai Tak Development

カイタック・ツインタワー | Hong Kong, China 2017

Work has begun on the major development of the former Kai Tak International Airport site in Hong Kong. The site is located in close proximity to Kowloon district and a new plan for a twin towers building is underway. The design requirements are as follows: the maximum building height is 120m and the required floor area is 100,000m^2; the lower floors accommodate a commercial facility and food court; the middle floors accommodate highly efficient rental offices; the higher floors accommodate the headquarter of the owner's company, and the central area of the site is an open central park. Rational planning and maintenance measures for structures and HVAC systems are the key to high-rise tower planning. A building core branching out in three stages is placed at the centre and the building, with structural grids extending from the building core was designed, creating an outline gradually spreading wider towards the ground with individual volumes transforming into different forms. The building volume is reduced on upper floors and the roof spaces are used for outdoor activities and also as an outdoor AC unit installation area allowing for easy maintenance.

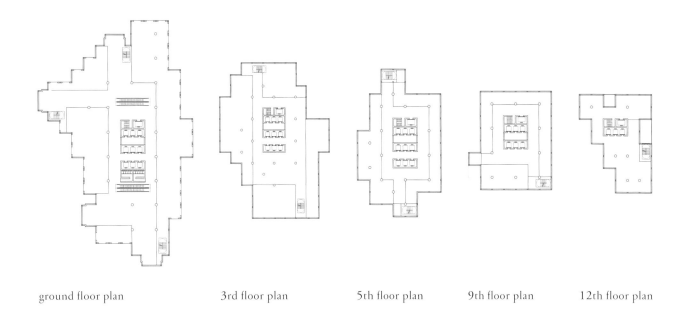

ground floor plan　　　　　3rd floor plan　　　　　5th floor plan　　　　　9th floor plan　　　　　12th floor plan

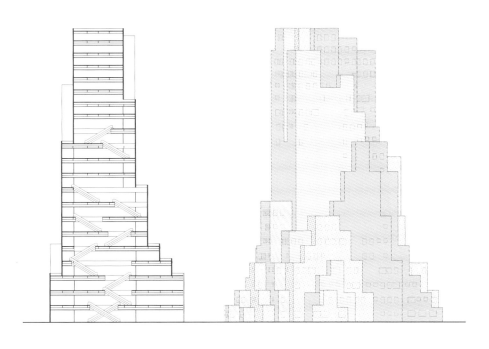

section - elevation　　　　　　　　　　　　　　　　　　　　　　　　　　　　　　　　　　　　　1/1500

香港島南東部の埋立地であるKai Tak（啓徳）国際空港跡地の大規模な開発が計画された。近隣には九龍地区があり、ここを官庁の施設やオフィス、商業施設などの計画が進むなか、市内からKai Tak地区へのゲートウェイとなる敷地にツインタワーの建設が立案された。建物は最高高120m、要求面積は約100,000m²あり、低層階に回遊性のある商業施設およびフードコート、中層階にはコンベンショナルなオフィス、高層階にオーナーの本社、敷地中央は中央公園がオープンスペースとして広がっている。高層タワーの計画においては構造と設備の合理性とメンテナンス性能が重要となる。中央に3段階に分岐していくコア機能を設け、そこから派生するようにグリッドを用いて下階にいくにつれ敷地周辺に向かって個々のボリュームが広がり、さまざまな形態に変容する建築とした。また建物上部はボリュームを減らすことで、トロピカルな熱帯環境として屋外利用する空間や、大気汚染の激しい香港の中で室外機などのメンテナンスや機器を容易に取り替えられる空間など、さまざまな屋外空間をつくることができる。

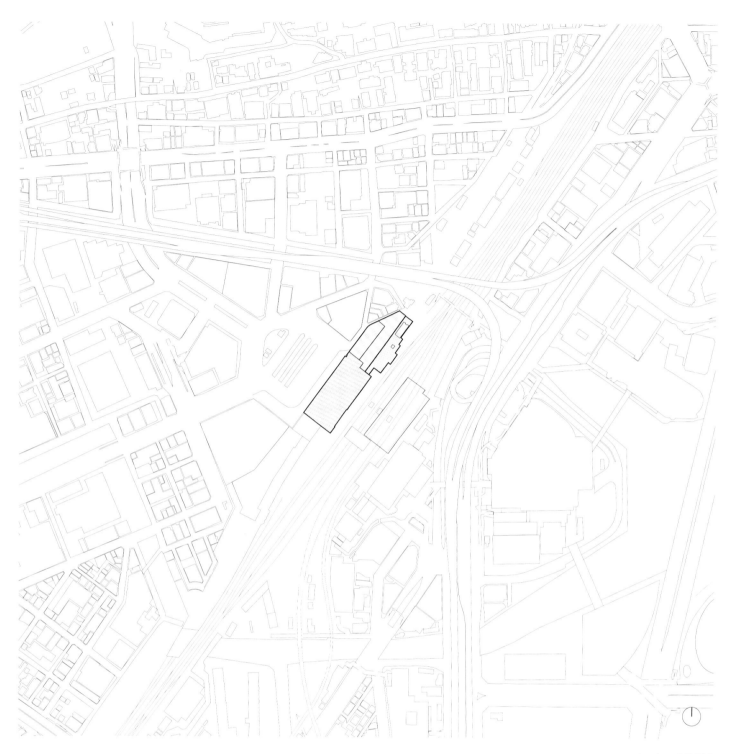

siteplan 1/5000

Yokohama Station Department Store

（仮称）横浜駅デパートメントストア | Yokohama, Japan 2016-

Yokohama Department Store is a commercial facility aiming to create lifestyles of a new era and local identity for Yokohama. We took inspiration from "bricks", a symbolic building material that created the history of Yokohama and conceived an idea of using tiles throughout the building. Tiles have been produced since ancient times and a wide variety of patterns, colors, and shapes provide infinite creative possibilities. Floors and walls from the first to tenth floors are entirely finished with tile collages depicting city maps, and internal public spaces are designed using different patterns and color tones. In terms of retail allocation, ten floors with a dimension of 174m in length and 48m in width, are to be divided into 200 tenant spaces. We are proposing shop layouts where spatial sequences unfold diagonally in section and circulation plans encourage shoppers to walk around in multiple directions and discover unexpected things, rather than completing circulation routes floor by floor. We are studying store plans where three store types, namely boutique stores (box type), market stores (open type), and pop-up stores (temporary type) are intermixed.

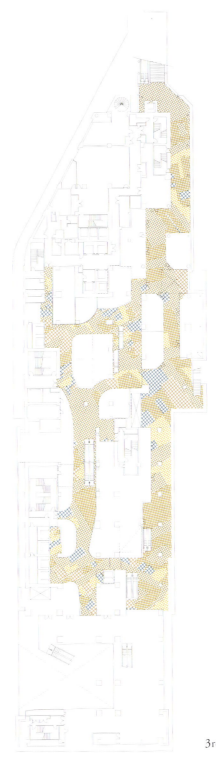

3rd floor plan　　　1/1000

（仮称）横浜駅デパートメントストアは新しい時代のライフスタイルと横浜の地域性を創り出すことを目指した商業施設である。横浜の歴史をつくりあげた「レンガ」から着想を得て、同じ土から生まれる素材である「タイル」を全面的に使う発想から始まった。「タイル」は古来より世界のどの地域でもつくられてきた素材であり、模様・色・形によって豊かな表現の可能性がある。そこで、1階から10階までの各階の床面と壁面を、都市の地図が描かれたタイルのコラージュで覆い尽くし、図式（パターン）と色調（トーン）による空間デザインがなされるように計画した。また、長さ174m、幅48mの幅が狭く奥行きのある細長い10層分の建物の中に約200店舗の区画が割り振られるため、吹き抜けを設け回遊性を斜めに発掘していく空間展開がされるような配置計画と、空間が多方向に広がるような散策と発見のある動線計画を行っている。店舗計画としては、ブティックストア（箱型）、マーケットストア（オープン型）、ポップアップストア（仮設型）の3タイプの店舗が混在する計画を試みている。

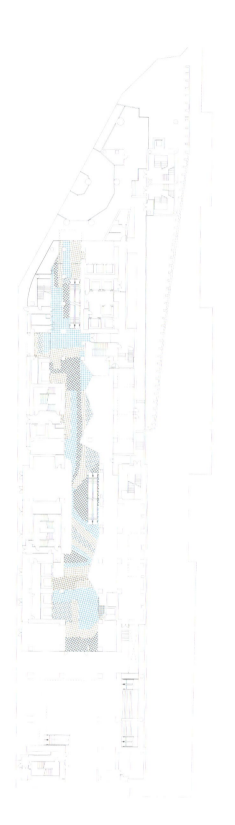

1st floor plan

2nd floor plan

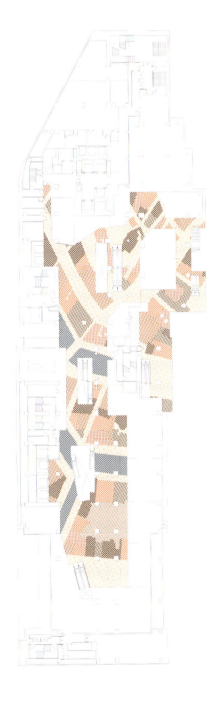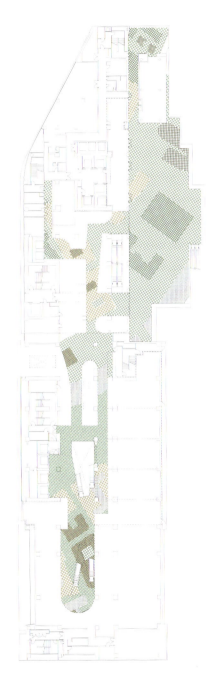

5th floor plan   6th floor plan   1/1000

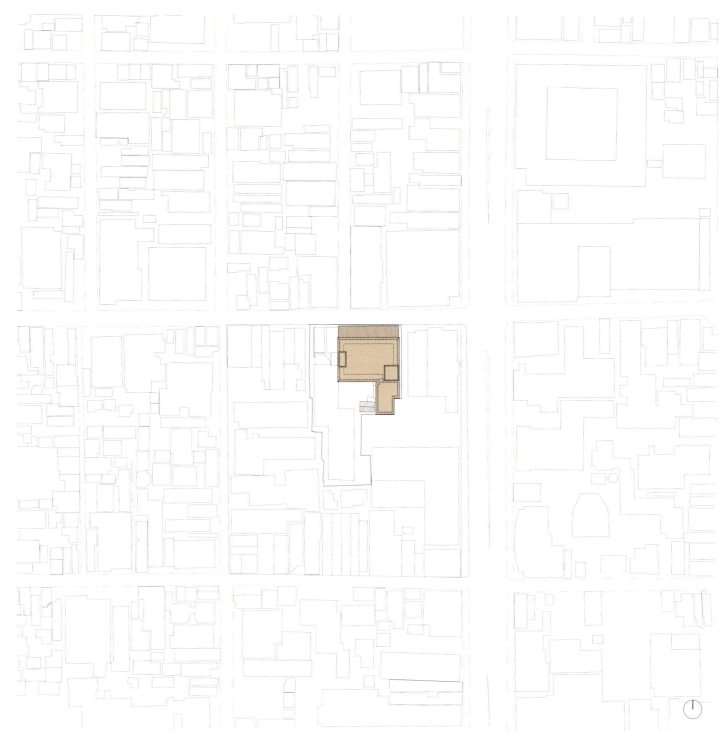

siteplan 1/2000

Chiso Building

千總本社ビル | Kyoto, Japan 2017-

Chiso Building is located along Sanjo-dori in Kyoto. This site has been successively inhabited since the 16th century by Chiso and our design intends to continue the refined atmosphere and prosperity of Sanjo-dori, the historical street is animated by commerce. The headquarter building completed in 1989 is set back from Sanjo-dori. Our proposed addition based on the scale of traditional Kyoto-style townhouses is intended to bring the building closer to Sanjo-dori, while its semi-open space under the eaves blurs the boundary between the building and the street. The structural frame of the existing building is preserved in the interior. This facility comprises shops serving as the Kimono headquarters in addition to a gallery and cafe. The interior spaces are articulated and connected using circular/curved lines and planes alleviating the rigid impression of the concrete structural grid. We intend to create a representational space using patterns and motifs with a sense of softness without hard edges. This project aims to transform the Chiso building into a cultural headquarter contributing to the development and promotion of kimono making and Japanese culture in Kyoto.

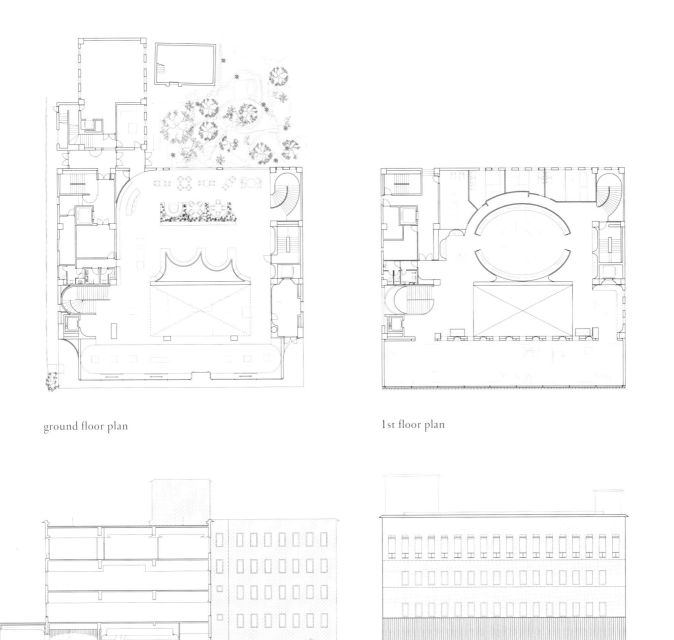

ground floor plan

1st floor plan

transversal section

north elevation   1/500

千總本社ビルは京都三条通りに面している。旧御所の一画ともいわれ、16世紀の室町時代から続くこの敷地に、歴史的に商業が栄えた京都三条通りの風情と賑わいを継承することから始めた。1989年に建てられた本社オフィスビルは三条通りからセットバックしているため、京町家のスケールに合わせた増築を行って三条通りとの距離を近づけながら、街並みを整え、半開放的な空間をつくることで境界線を曖昧にしようとしている。また内部には既存の建物の構造躯体を残し、地下階から2階まで3層分は「和装本舗」の店舗を中心とし、ギャラリーやカフェも含む和文化の伝統と未来を担う施設となる。各階にはRC造のグリッド空間に対して円形やR型のような曲線や曲面による分節と連結を挿入していくことで全体に和らぎが感じられる空間としている。また硬い質感ではなく、柔らかな質感を用いて図柄や模様による表象空間の創出を試みている。千總の本社オフィスビルから、未来の京都の和文化を担う着物づくりの本舗へと発展させる計画となる。

siteplan 1/1000

A House for Oiso

A House for Oiso | Kanagawa, Japan 2014-15

The site in Oiso is located on a hillside overlooking the sea toward the south and is surrounded by mountains on the north side. Since this land was not affected by land development, serene landscapes with lush greenery and undulating roads are preserved. Under the building code of Japan, the building coverage ratio is specified but the building placement is decided at individual discretion, and as a result, streetscapes often become irregular. Considering this, we conceived an idea of integrating the house and the land by returning 50% of the site back to the ground of Oiso and use the remaining 50% to build a house. The first floor comprises small structures called "*muro*" (room) each accommodating a vestibule, bathroom, tatami room, and kitchen and an "*ima*" (living room) located in the center. An idea of living environment, the second floor accommodating "*nema*" (sleeping space), the origin of home, is raised above the ground. The ground was excavated by 60cm and the excavated earth was used to finish the interior and exterior. Because the earth finish effectively absorbs excess moisture and stabilizes the room temperature, the house is constantly cool in summer and warm in winter.

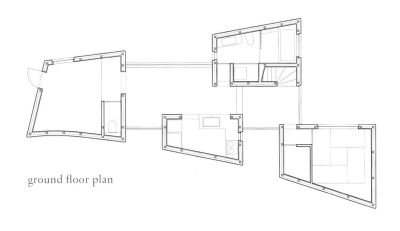

ground floor plan

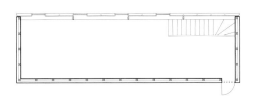

1st floor plan

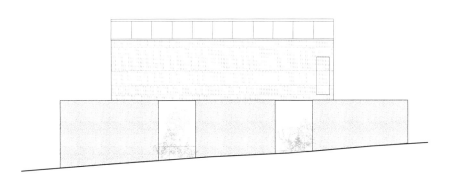

east elevation   1/200

東京から約1時間ほどの場所にある大磯の敷地は、北面が山に囲まれ、南面が海に向かって広がるなだらかな丘陵地である。宅地開発がされなかったため、多くの緑に囲まれ、古い山に沿ってできた道が穏やかな風景をつくっている。しかし昨今では分譲化が進み、建物の配置計画が個人に委ねられているため、土地の利用方法によってまち並みにバラつきが生まれやすい。そこで、家を土地の形状に合わせて50%の床面積を確保し、50%は大磯の土地に還元して家と大地の一体化を試みた。1階は、前室・浴室・和室・台所による「室（ムロ）」の小さな構造体を集めて全体を安定させ、中央には暮らしの場として、家族や人が集まる土に覆われた「イマ（居間）」を設けた。そして本来の家である「ネマ（寝間）」を地面からもち上げ、2階は木に包まれる眠りの場とした。また家全体の環境計画として、床面を地面から60cmほど掘り込み、その土を使って外壁、内壁、床のすべてを土地の土で覆った。土が湿気を吸い湿度を安定させるため、夏は涼しく、床下の熱源が地面を温めるため、冬はあたたかい環境を保つことができる。

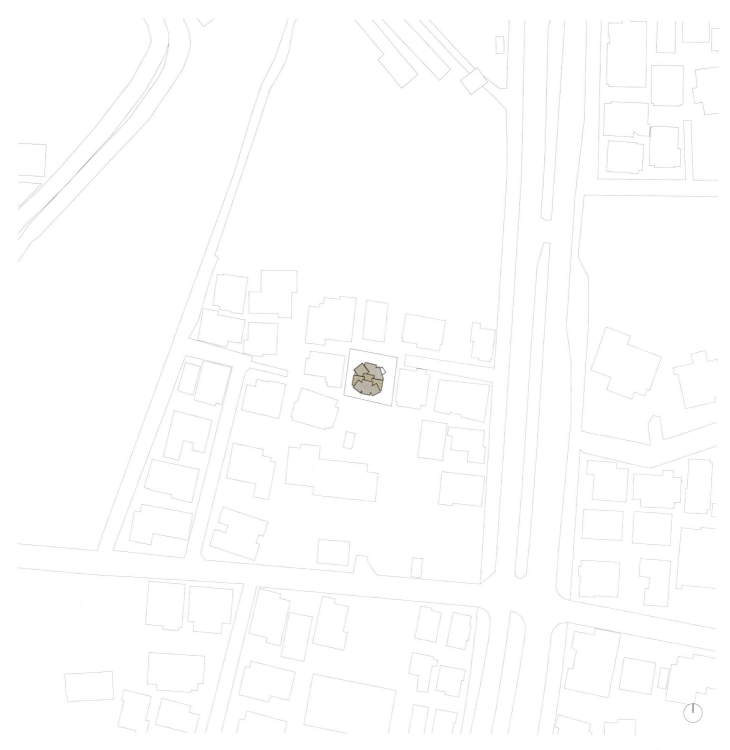

siteplan 1/1000

Todoroki House in Valley

Todoroki House in Valley | Tokyo, Japan 2017-18

The site is located in a built-up residential area where the existing forest in the valley was cleared and developed into housing lots. The first floor is a 4.2-m high space embedded in the sloping ground and surrounded by lush forest. We designed the octagonal floor plan that creates a space that is simultaneously open and enclosed. The second floor is comprised of eight volumes branching out into different directions and connected at the center to form a single space. The third-floor space accommodating a children's room is tall and narrow. The building volume is extended up to the maximum eave height imposed by the set-back regulation, constituting a building that goes into the earth, up through the trees, and out to the sky. The foundations are constructed of reinforced concrete and the building is wood structure partially reinforced with steel beams. In order to open the building towards the forest on the south side, 90% of the dead load is carried by a wall on the north side and two wall-columns are provided to resist seismic loads. We studied the surrounding forest and planted more than fifty species of plants to create a forest integrated with the existing trees and plants.

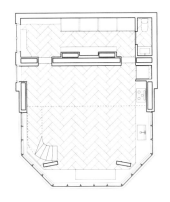

ground floor plan

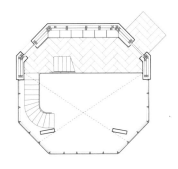

1st floor plan

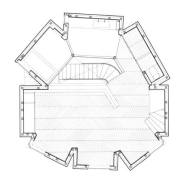

2nd floor plan

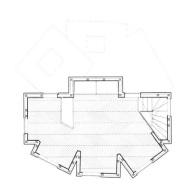

3rd floor plan

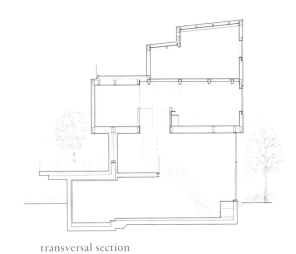

transversal section

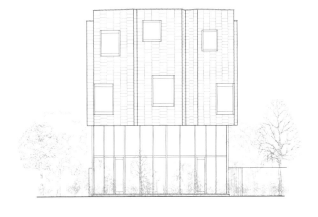

south elevation   1/200

敷地周辺は渓谷の森林が伐採され分譲地として開発された住宅地であり、周辺は密集した住宅に囲まれていた。家の1階は地中に埋め込み、森に覆われたような天井高4.2mの大空間でありながら洞窟のような落ち着きある空間となり、八角形の平面によって包まれながらも開かれた状態となっている。一方、主寝室と浴室がある2階は多方向に分岐する8つのボリュームが集まることで連結した空間となり、子ども部屋のある3階は床面の奥行きをぐっと小さくしながらも天井を高くした。北側斜線ギリギリの最高軒高までボリュームを立ち上げ、土の中から木の間を抜けて空へとつながるような構成とした。 建物は基礎部分のみコンクリート造とし、全体は木構造で組まれ一部鉄骨の梁により補強されている。1階を南面の森へと開放するため、建物の約90%の自重は北側の壁面で支えられ、2本の壁柱は地震力を受けるために設けられている。また「都会の大自然」をつくるという施主のコンセプトを基に、近隣の森を観察しながら世界各地の樹木や草木50種類以上を植えたことで、等々力の植生と混ざり合い、森の一部となった。

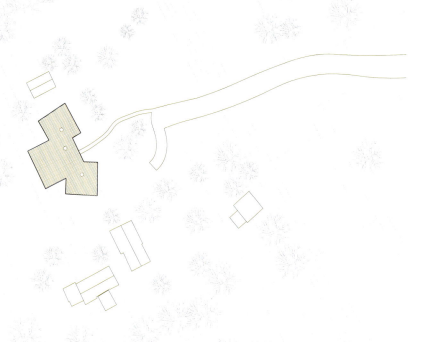

siteplan 1/1000

Weekend House in Fontainebleau

フォンテーヌブロー週末住宅 | Fontainebleau, France 2017-

The Forest of Fontainebleau is an expansive forest with an area of 17,000 hectares. Our client requested us to design a weekend house where the family could spend the weekend with friends enjoying nature. The Forest of Fontainebleau is the world's first designated nature reserve. The site is surrounded by forests, but has an open grassland on the south side, and overlooks a valley with forest beyond. We arrived at a combination of three volumes respectively interacting with the forest. The central volume contains an open space with an 11m-wide glazed opening directly connected to the trees: the interior space reflects any change that happens in the forest. There are no supporting columns, and sloped roofs and warped ceilings accentuate the spatial composition. The three interconnected volumes are wrapped in freeform-curved walls. The eave height of each volume is set at a different level in relation to the ground and its distance to the surrounding forest, so that the exterior harmonizes with the landscape while connecting each of the interior spaces with its surrounding landscapes in all directions and in various ways.

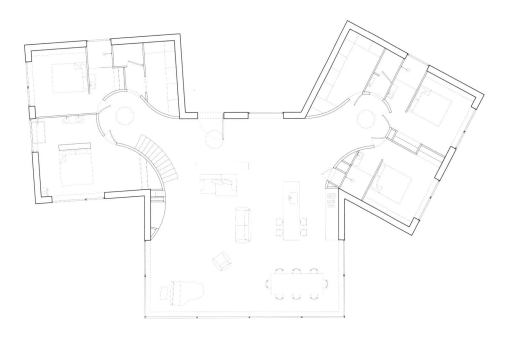

ground floor plan

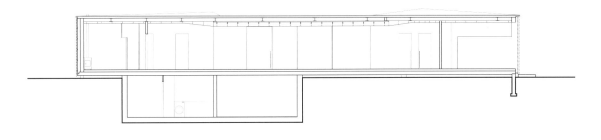

longitudinal section

1/200

フォンテーヌブローの森はパリから約60kmの距離にあり約17,000haの森が広がっている。自然に囲まれながら家族や友人と過ごすための週末住宅を建てたいという要望から、このプロジェクトは始まった。フォンテーヌブローの森は世界で最初に保護されたユネスコの自然遺産地区であり、周囲は森林に囲まれ、南面のみ開かれた草地が広がり、その先は谷間となり広大な森が広がる。さまざまな形式や形態のスタディを行った後、3つのボリュームがそれぞれで周囲の森と呼応するようなアイデアが生まれた。中央のボリュームはオープンスペースとして幅11mのガラス面が森に向かって開かれ、時間の変化とともに外の森と内の空間とが変化していく。構造的に柱はなく、屋根面の傾きと天井面を湾曲させることで、そこに空間的な抑揚が生まれる。また3つのボリュームが連結し、それらをつなぐ壁面はゆるやかな自由曲線によって包まれるような平面となっている。単純な3つのボリュームの軒高位置を、敷地の高低差と周囲の森林との距離によってそれぞれ変えることで、外側では風景との調和へと、内側からは多方向で多角的な空間と風景との切り取りへとつながりをつくろうとしている。

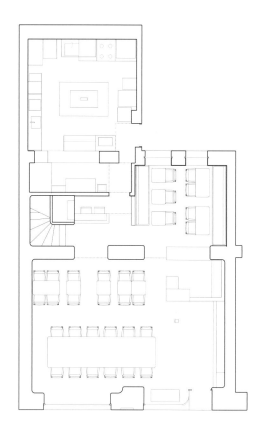

plan 1/150

Toraya Paris

とらやパリ店 | Paris, France 2015

TORAYA Paris, the Paris branch of TORAYA, has been loved by Parisians since 1980. We were requested to update its impression and create a space integrating Japanese and Paris culture. Our design started from dividing the shop interior into three zones. The large table placed in front of the window is inspired by the cafe culture in Paris. The central zone is a tearoom where customers can enjoy the space with a sense of softness and the rear zone is a salon with a calm atmosphere where one feels as if one is sitting inside a *kashigata* (wood mold for Japanese sweets). The wood walls are made of French oak scraped perpendicular to the grain. Travertine is laid out in small pieces to even out stone grain. Troweled plaster finish was applied to the interior so that all corners are smoothed out and light and shadow seamlessly connect in gradations. All furniture pieces are custom-made and TORAYA's crest called *kantora* is used as a design motif. At each corner, adjoining components harmoniously connect through "*oriai*" (mutual concessions), which is a unique presentation of the Japanese culture of "*wa*" (harmony and compassion) only possible in this special space.

とらやパリ店は1980年にオープンして以来、パリ市民から長年にわたって大切にされてきた店舗である。当初から同じ面積でありながら改装によりイメージを刷新し、新たに「和の文化」と「パリの文化」が融合するような空間が求められた。まず店舗内を3つのゾーニングでゆるやかに振り分け、通りに近い窓辺には大テーブルを設けることで、人びとが寄り添いながら楽しむパリのカフェ文化のような席とした。中央は柔らかな空間を楽しむティールーム座席とし、奥には木型に包まれるような落ち着いたサロン座席を設けた。素材のフレンチオークは木目を出すために横引きで粗く削り出し、トラバーチンは細かく石を切り出して石目をならした。天井や壁や床の角のすべての境目をぼかして光と影が柔らかくつながるように手仕事の痕跡を残す漆喰の仕上げとした。家具はすべてオリジナルで制作され、とらやの紋である「鐶虎（かんとら）」をモチーフとした。それぞれの角が「折り合い」によって調和を生み、和の文化をパリで伝える、パリにしかない特別なとらやの空間が実現した。

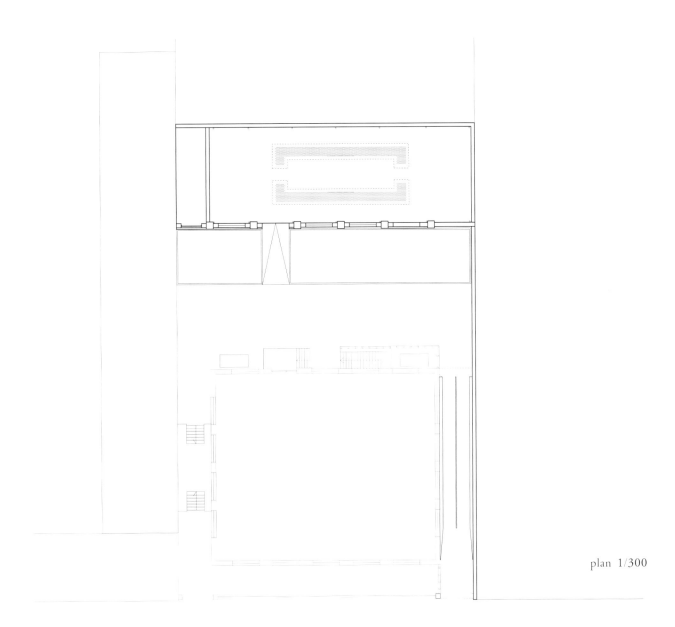

plan 1/300

Luce Tempo Luogo

Luce Tempo Luogo | Milan, Italy 2011

In 2011, TOSHIBA presented an exhibition introducing new possibilities for LED lights at Milan Design Week. At Cortile di Via Savona in Zona Tortona, there is an alleyway leading to a courtyard facing the wall of a ruined building. We conceived an idea of dividing the existing space into three zones, namely "line", "surface", and "volume" to create a site-specific installation. line: "A line of light." A cave with a 10-mm wide "line of light" along the center of the ceiling is built. A line of light splits in two through a reflection of light on a strip of water running along the center of the floor. surface: "A surface of light." A water surface is created in front of the wall. During the day, sunlit ripple patterns change along with the movement of the sun. At night, the ripples lit with LEDs create ripples of light on the wall. volume: "A volume of light." The duration of lighting is program-controlled. Falling waterdrops transform into light particles when illuminated by light with the duration of 5/1,000,000 second. When the duration of light is 2000/1,000,000 second, particles of light become lines of light and thus light is visualized as time.

東芝の創業者である藤岡市助はエジソンから学び日本で初めて白熱電球を製造した。100年が経ち白熱電球の製造を中止し、新たにLEDの可能性をミラノデザインウィークで発表した。会場はトルトーナ地区の既存の建物の間の細い路地を抜けた、屋根も壊れた廃墟の壁だけが残る中庭。その名もなき壁に惹かれ、この場所を3つの空間に分け、LED光による サイトスペシフィックなインスタレーションを行うことにした。①line＝光の線。中央に幅10mmの光の線によるシームレスな光の洞窟をつくる。中央の床の水の線の反射によって、光の線は1本から2本の線となる。②surface＝光の面。壁の前に水面を設置し、太陽の動きとともに光の波紋が刻々と変わる。夜は高輝度LEDにより水面の波紋が光となって壁面に浮かび上がる。③volume＝光の量。光の発光時間をプログラミングする。最短で100万分の5秒の光を水滴に照射すると光は点となる。そこから光の時間を100万分の2,000秒の光に変換すると光は点から線へと変化し、光を時間として可視化させる。

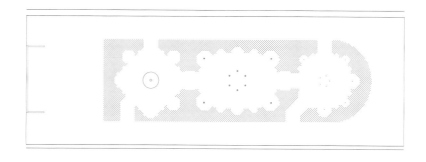

plan

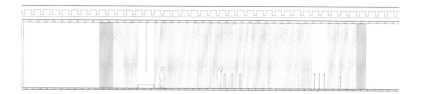

section 1/300

LIGHT is TIME

LIGHT is TIME | Milan, Italy 2014

CITIZEN is a Japanese watch maker founded in 1918 based on the company philosophy to create "watches for all citizens." In 2014, CITIZEN held the first exhibition at the Triennale di Milano Exhibition and chose the Triennale Design Museum as the venue. About 80,000 watch base plates are categorized into 36 types and were suspended from the ceiling using over 4,000 pieces of wire to form a space. We gave precise instructions including the location and height of respective patterns, while intending to combine the sublimity of continuous order and the fragmented chaos or disorder. In addition, the 4,000 pieces of wire shine and keep moving in sync with light and sounds generated through programming, using random numbers as an expression of the existence of endless time. Three exhibition spaces with the themes "Origin", "Parts", and "Watches" were located in the center of the spatial installation at the venue. LIGHT is TIME. A successive exhibition celebrating the success was held at Spiral Hall in Tokyo in the autumn of the same year, followed by another exhibition at the Cloister of Bramante (Rome) in 2018.

シチズンは「すべての市民のために時計を」という想いとともに1918年に創業した日本の時計メーカーである。2014年に初めてミラノサローネに出展し、ミラノ市内の中心にあるデザインの殿堂、トリエンナーレ美術館を会場に選んだ。約80,000枚の基盤装置を数学的比率によるパターンで36種類の類型に分類し、それらを約4,000本のワイヤーで吊るすことによって空間を構成した。天井から床のどの位置にどのパターンが設置されるかまで設計を行い、連続的な秩序による崇高さと、断片的で無秩序にも見える混沌とした状態を同居させた。さらに乱数を含んだプログラメーションによって発せられる光と音によって空間全体が煌めき、揺らぎ、動き続けることで、止まることのない空間と時間を体験することとなる。またインスタレーションの中央部には「Origin＝始まり」「Parts＝部品と意味」「Watches＝時代と時計」の3つのテーマで空間を設定し、展示を行った。このLIGHT is TIMEは同年秋には凱旋展として東京・表参道のスパイラルホールで、また2018年にはローマのブラマンテの回廊（キオストロ・デル・ブラマンテ）でも展示された。

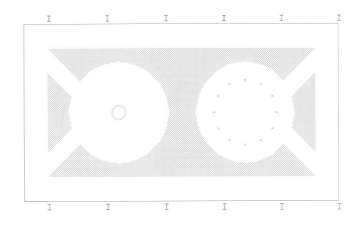

plan

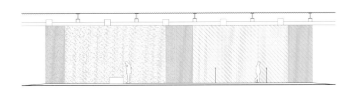

section 1/300

time is TIME

time is TIME | Milan, Italy 2016

We selected a 800m² warehouse-like space as the venue for the 2016 CITIZEN exhibition in Milan and converted it into a space sandwiched between two aluminum plates. Two circular-shaped open spaces were enclosed in square-shaped spaces, and the spaces around the circles were filled with 120,000 watch main plates suspended from the ceiling using 8,000 pieces of wire to create installations respectively entitled "organic time" and "systematic time." While "organic time" space offered a spatial experience where main plates, light, and sound were placed in sequence organically, "systematic time" space offered an austere and intermittent spatial experience where main plates, light, and sound were organized geometrically. All exhibits were based on the theme of "one second." In the "organic time" space, sixty mechanical watches continually indicated only "seconds", with their second hands continually moving. In the "systematic time" space, twelve themes related to time, including "cell time", "emotion time", "rotating time & revolving time" were conceived. Experimental watches used to measure "one second" under these time themes were developed and displayed.

2016年、2度目となるシチズンのミラノデザインウィークの展示会場は800m²の倉庫のような空間を選んだ。そこに天井と床に水平な2枚の面で挟み込む実験的な空間を設えた。入れ子状に開放されたふたつの正円形空間の周りに、約8,000本のワイヤーによって固定された約120,000枚の「地板（じいた）」と呼ばれる基盤装置によって埋め尽くす空間をつくり、「organic time」と「systematic time」を並置するインスタレーションとした。「organic time」では有機的な空間体験として地板や光や音が有機的に連続するのに対し、「systematic time」は厳格で非連続的な空間体験として地板や光や音も幾何学的に離散的に構成される空間となる。双方の空間は隣接しながらも、両方を同時には絶対に経験できない「時空間」を体感するインスタレーションとなった。また展示物のすべては「秒」をテーマに構成され、時間を「1秒」で観測することによって起こる、さまざまなミクロやマクロな地球と宇宙の計測装置として実験時計の開発の展示を行った。

Timeline
2004-2027

Line of Tears – Sumatra Tsunami Memorial *
status: competition
location: Oslo, Norway
date: 2006
program: installation

Umm el-Fahem Contemporary Art Museum *
status: competition
location: Umm el-Fahem, Israel
date: 2007
area: 9,000 m²
program: museum

2004

SHIKAKU, Noism
status: completed
location: Niigata, Japan
date: 2004
area: 200 m²
program: scenography
photo: Kishin Shinoyama

minä perhonen 2007 S/S Fashion Show *
status: completed
location: Paris, France
date: 2006
area: 182 m²
program: scenography
photo: Koomi Kim

Johnny Farah Boutique *
status: completed
location: Paris, France
date: 2007
area: 100 m²
program: interior design

2006

2007

2008

Estonian National Museum *
status: international competition | 1st prize
location: Tartu, Estonia
date: 2006
area: 34,581 m²
program: museum

PLAY 2 PLAY – *interfering dimension*, Noism *
status: completed
location: Niigata, Japan
date: 2007
area: 200 m²
program: scenography
photo: Kishin Shinoyama

MIHARAYASUHIRO 2008 A/W Fashion Show *
status: completed
location: Paris, France
date: 2008
area: 450 m²
program: scenography

New Silk Road – Pavilion for Cultural Park *
status: international competition | shortlisted
location: Xi'an, China
date: 2006
area: 16,000 m²
program: pavilion

Line of Voices – Open-air Theatre *
status: competition | 2nd prize
location: Riga, Latvia
date: 2007
area: 14,000 m²
program: theatre

Bodo City Platform *
status: competition
location: Bodø, Norway
date: 2008
area: 162,000 m²
program: complex

2009

Cartlon Groves *
status: competition
location: Beirut, Lebanon
date: 2008
area: 30,000 m²
program: apartment block

52 Ludlow *
status: project
location: Milan, Italy
date: 2008
area: 153 m²
program: exhibition design

Té TO Té, Ballet National de Marseille *
status: completed
location: Marseille, France
date: 2008
area: 200 m²
program: scenography

At one end of the corner (with film "Kinecalligraph" by Kiyoji Otsuji, Yasuhiro Ishimoto and Saiko Tsuji), Taka Ishii Gallery, Frieze *
status: completed
location: London, UK
date: 2008
area: 5 m²
program: installation
photo: Courtesy of Taka Ishii Gallery

Wonderground – Natural History Museum of Denmark *
status: international competition
location: Copenhagen, Denmark
date: 2009
area: 15,000 m²
program: museum

A Beacon of Light *
status: competition | honorable mention
location: Beirut, Lebanon
date: 2009
area: 17,000 m²
program: complex

Jazdow Stories – Polish History Museum *
status: competition
location: Warsaw, Poland
date: 2009
area: 21,000 m²
program: museum

Malpensa Airport Gate *
status: international competition
location: Milan, Italy
date: 2009
area: 1,125 m²
program: renovation

MKH Tabaris Tower *
status: project
location: Beirut, Lebanon
date: 2009
area: 28,000 m²
program: complex

Preston Meadow *
status: competition
location: Preston, UK
date: 2009
area: 1,155 m²
program: apartment block

Landscape Stories – Polish History Museum *
status: competition
location: Warsaw, Poland
date: 2009
area: 20,000 m²
program: museum

I-CON – Shenzhen & Hong Kong Bi-City Biennale of Urbanism and Architecture *
status: international competition
location: Shenzen, China
date: 2009
program: pavilion

Zone / academic, Noism *
status: completed
location: Niigata, Japan
date: 2009
area: 200 m²
program: scenography
photo: Takashi Shikama

Zone / nomadic, Noism *
status: completed
location: Niigata, Japan
date: 2009
area: 200 m²
program: scenography
photo: Takashi Shikama

minä perhonen rooms *
status: completed
location: Tilburg, the Netherlands
date: 2009
area: 182 m²
program: exhibition design

2010

Pasts
status: completed
location: Tokyo, Japan
date: 2010
program: installation
photo: Courtesy of Taka Ishii Gallery

Metropolis *
status: project
location: undisclosed
date: 2010
area: 200,000 m²
program: complex

A Quarry for Diamonds *
status: international competition | shortlisted
location: Beirut, Lebanon
date: 2010
area: 59,000 m²
program: complex

Russian Orthodox Cultural and Spritual Centre *
status: international competition
location: Paris, France
date: 2010
area: 4,200 m²
program: church

2011

Ishinomaki Reconstruction *
status: project
location: Ishinomaki, Japan
date: 2011-13
program: urban design research
collaboration: GRAU

Beirut Village *
status: project
location: Hazmieh, Lebanon
date: 2011
area: 7,000 m²
program: apartment block

Luce Tempo Luogo, Toshiba in Milano Salone *
status: completed
location: Milan, Italy
date: 2011
area: 534 m²
program: installation
photo: Francesco Niki Takehiko

Bluebeard's, Saito Kinen Festival Matsumoto *
status: completed
location: Matsumoto, Japan
date: 2011
area: 250 m²
program: scenography
photo: Kishin Shinoyama

The Miraculous Mandarin, Saito Kinen Festival Matsumoto *
status: completed
location: Matsumoto, Japan
date: 2011
area: 250 m²
program: scenography
photo: Kishin Shinoyama

2012

Kofun Stadium – New National Stadium Japan *
status: international competition | finalist
location: Tokyo, Japan
date: 2012
area: 290,000 m²
program: stadium
collaboration: A+ Architecture"

Arthur Rimbaud Museum *
status: competition | 2nd prize
location: Charleville-Mézières, France
date: 2012
area: 520 m²
program: museum

Velodrome Maspes-Vigorelli *
status: international competition | shortlisted
location: Milan, Italy
date: 2012
area: 6,311 m²
program: stadium

Maspero Apartment *
status: completed
location: Paris, France
date: 2012
area: 250 m²
program: interior design
photo: Takuji Shimmura

The Bump, Renault in Paris Motorshow *
status: completed
location: Paris, France
date: 2012
area: 4,312 m²
program: pavilion
photo: Takuji Shimmura

365 Charming Everyday Things *
status: completed
location: Paris, France
date: 2012
area: 629 m²
program: exhibition design
photo: Takuji Shimmura

2013

Padiglione Italia Expo *
status: international competition
location: Milan, Italy
date: 2013
area: 12,000 m²
program: pavilion

Broussais *
status: competition
location: Paris, France
date: 2013
area: 4,900 m²
program: apartment block

Frozen Time, Citizen in Baselworld *
status: completed
location: Basel, Switzerland
date: 2013
area: 147 m²
program: installation
photo: Takuji Shimmura

ARAI Junichi Tradition and Creation *
status: completed
location: Tokyo, Japan
date: 2013
area: 900 m²
program: exhibition design
photo: Keizo Kioku

Taka Ishii Gallery in Paris Photo *
status: completed
location: Paris, France
date: 2013
area: 60 m²
program: exhibition design
photo: Takuji Shimmura

2014

IPES Public Office Building *
status: international competition | 1st prize
location: Bolzano, Italy
date: 2014
area: 8,500 m²
program: office building

Hokusai in Grand Palais *
status: completed
location: Paris, France
date: 2014
area: 1,500 m²
program: exhibition design
photo: Takuji Shimmura

LIGHT is TIME, Citizen in Milano Salone *
status: completed
location: Milan, Italy
date: 2014
area: 423 m²
program: installation
photo: Takuji Shimmura

archaeological future in wood and color *
status: completed
location: Tokyo, Japan
date: 2014
area: 80 m²
program: product design
photo: Amazon Kajiyama

Compressed Time, Citizen in Baselworld *
status: completed
location: Basel, Switzerland
date: 2014
area: 147 m²
program: installation
photo: HIROBA

Hermès Shoes Pop-up Store *
status: completed
location: Tokyo, Japan
date: 2014
area: 24 m²
program: interior design
photo: Nacása & Partners Inc. | Courtesy of Hermès Japon

2015

eComachine *
status: international competition
location: Paris, France
date: 2015
area: 125,000 m²
program: complex

Taka Ishii Gallery Photography Paris *
status: completed
location: Paris, France
date: 2014
area: 80 m²
program: interior design
photo: Takuji Shimmura

Ginza Maison Hermès Window Display *
status: completed
location: Tokyo, Japan
date: 2014
area: 8 m²
program: window display
photo: Satoshi Asakawa | Courtesy of Hermès Japon

Shibuya Department Store *
status: international competition | shortlisted
location: Tokyo, Japan
date: 2015
area: 32,000 m²
program: complex

Taka Ishii Gallery in Paris Photo *
status: completed
location: Paris, France
date: 2014
area: 60 m²
program: exhibition design
photo: Takuji Shimmura

Hear My Sole, Kaz Kumagai *
status: completed
location: Tokyo, Japan
date: 2014
area: 200 m²
program: scenography

New Science Centre of Naples *
status: international competition | 3rd prize
location: Naples, Italy
date: 2015
area: 10,000 m²
program: museum

Yokohama Building *
status: completed
location: Kanagawa, Japan
date: 2014-15
area: 7,802 m²
program: office building
collaboration: Ondesign
photo: koichi torimura

Kanazawa in Ginza *
status: completed
location: Tokyo, Japan
date: 2015
area: 310 m²
program: interior design
photo: Takumi Ota

Expansion Time, Citizen in Baselworld *
status: completed
location: Basel, Switzerland
date: 2015
area: 147 m²
program: installation
photo: Takuji Shimmura

A House for Oiso *
status: completed
location: Kanagawa, Japan
date: 2014-15
area: 122 m²
program: house
photo: Takumi Ota

Architect Frank Gehry "I Have an Idea" *
status: completed
location: Tokyo, Japan
date: 2015
area: 726 m²
program: exhibition design
photo: Keizo Kioku

Piaget in Watches & Wonders *
status: completed
location: Hong Kong, China
date: 2015
area: 400 m²
program: installation
photo: Piaget

Toraya Paris *
status: completed
location: Paris, France
date: 2015
area: 230 m²
program: interior design
photo: Takuji Shimmura

1∞ MINAKAKERU *
status: completed
location: Tokyo, Japan
date: 2015
area: 600 m²
program: exhibition design
photo: Takumi Ota

LIGHT in WATER *
status: completed
location: Paris, France
date: 2015
area: 170 m²
program: installation

Chiso Building *
status: completed
location: Kyoto, Japon
date: 2015
area: 500 m²
program: interior design
photo: OMOTE Nobutada

1∞ MINAKAKERU – Past and Future of minä perhonen *
status: completed
location: Nagasaki, Japan
date: 2015
area: 984 m²
program: exhibition design
photo: Takumi Ota

Amana in Paris Photo *
status: completed
location: Paris, France
date: 2015
area: 60 m²
program: exhibition design
photo: Takuji Shimmura

Taka Ishii Gallery in Paris Photo *
status: completed
location: Paris, France
date: 2015
area: 68 m²
program: exhibition design
photo: Takuji Shimmura

AFEX 2016 *
status: completed
location: Paris, France
date: 2016
area: 600 m²
program: exhibition design
photo: AFEX

Taka Ishii Gallery in Paris Photo *
status: completed
location: Paris, France
date: 2016
area: 60 m²
program: exhibition design
photo: Takuji Shimmura

YCAM - Yoko Ando "Dividual Plays —
Dialogue between the unconscious and systems" *
status: completed
location: Yamaguchi, Japan
date: 2015
area: 150 m²
program: space design
photo: work in progress of the piece by Ryuichi Maruo (YCAM)
Courtesy of Yamaguchi Center for Arts and Media [YCAM]

Urban Theatre – Beirut Museum of Art *
status: international competition
location: Beirut, Lebanon
date: 2016
area: 15,000 m²
program: museum

Jardins, Musée du Luxembourg Exhibition *
status: competition
location: Paris, France
date: 2016
area: 550 m²
program: exhibition design

Vogue Japan Women of the Year 2015 Trophy *
status: completed
location: Tokyo, Japan
date: 2015
program: object

The Japan Store Isetan Mitsukoshi *
status: completed
location: Paris, France
date: 2016
area: 90 m²
program: interior design
photo: Takuji Shimmura

Piaget – SIHH 2016 *
status: completed
location: Geneva, Switzerland
date: 2016
area: 150 m²
program: installation
photo: Piaget

2016

Estonian National Museum *
status: completed
location: Tartu, Estonia
date: 2006-16
area: 34,581 m²
program: museum
photo: Eesti Rahva Muuseum

Masterpieces from the Centre Pompidou: Timeline 1906-1977 *
status: completed
location: Tokyo, Japan
date: 2016
area: 1,930 m²
program: exhibition design
photo: The Asahi Shimbun

time is TIME, Citizen in Milano Salone *
status: completed
location: Milan, Italy
date: 2016
area: 800 m²
program: installation
photo: Takuji Shimmura

Piaget – SIHH 2017 *
status: project
location: Geneva, Switzerland
date: 2016
area: 150 m²
program: installation
photo: Piaget

Parts to the Furniture, Asahikawa Design Week *
status: completed
location: Asahiawa, Japan
date: 2016
area: 150 m²
program: installation
photo: Yutaka Endo - LUFTZUG

Horizontal Time, Citizen in Baselworld *
status: completed
location: Basel, Switzerland
date: 2016
area: 147 m²
program: installation
photo: Takuji Shimmura

Chiso Installation *
status: completed
location: Kuala Lumpur, Malaysia
date: 2016
area: 12 m²
program: installation

La Bayadere – nation of illusion, Noism *
status: completed
location: Niigata, Japan
date: 2016
area: 200 m²
program: scenography
photo: Kishin Shinoyama

2017

Twin Towers in Kai Tak Development
status: international competition | shortlisted
location: Hong Kong, China
date: 2017
area: 100,000 m²
program: complex
photo: Frans Parthesius

Kyoto City University of Arts, Kyoto City Dohda Senior High School of Art
status: international competition
location: Kyoto, Japan
date: 2017
area: 63,000 m²
program: university and high school
collaboration: SANDWICH, Shin Takamatsu Architect and Associates, Kume Sekkei

Kukio Villa
status: competition
location: Hawaii, USA
date: 2017
area: 250 m²
program: house

Kyomachiya Hotel Shiki Juraku
status: completed
location: Kyoto, Japan
date: 2017
area: 37 m²
program: renovation
photo: Yuna Yagi

Clé de Peau Beauté – GSIX
status: completed
location: Tokyo, Japan
date: 2017
area: 85 m²
program: interior design
photo: Taihei Iino

The Harvest 2017
status: completed
location: Akita, Japan
date: 2017
program: product design

2018

Tokyo Future
status: project
location: Tokyo, Japan
date: 2018
program: urban design research

Todoroki House in Valley
status: completed
location: Tokyo, Japan
date: 2017-18
area: 188 m²
program: house
photo: Yuna Yagi

Time Théâtre, Citizen in Baselworld
status: completed
location: Basel, Switzerland
date: 2018
area: 1,315 m²
program: installation
photo: HIROBA

Restaurant Maison
status: ongoing
location: Paris, France
date: 2017-
area: 293 m²
program: restaurant

Japonism 2018 – Information Centre
status: completed
location: Paris, France
date: 2018
area: 90 m²
program: interior design

Balthus Chapel
status: ongoing
location: Rossinière, Switzerland
date: 2018-
area: 58 m²
program: chapel

Furoshiki Paris
status: ongoing
location: Paris, France
date: 2018-
area: 500 m²
program: pavilion

Tsuyoshi Tane | Archaeology of the Future – Digging & Building
status: completed
location: Tokyo, Japan
date: 2018
area: 900 m²
program: exhibition design

Tsuyoshi Tane | Archaeology of the Future – Search & Research
status: completed
location: Tokyo, Japan
date: 2018
area: 200 m²
program: exhibition design

A gaze into architecture – Phases of Contemporary Photography and Architecture
status: completed
location: Tokyo, Japan
date: 2018
area: 150 m²
program: exhibition design

2019

Weekend House in Fontainebleau
status: ongoing
location: Fontainebleau, France
date: 2017-
area: 300 m²
program: house
photo: Frans Parthesius

29th Floor Show Room at Empire State Building
status: ongoing
location: New York, USA
date: 2018-
area: 150 m²
program: interior design
photo: Sam valadi, CC BY 2.0

Cité Griset Renovation
status: ongoing
location: Paris, France
date: 2018-
area: 1,250 m²
program: interior design

Luxembourg Apartment
status: ongoing
location: Paris, France
date: 2018-
area: 230 m²
program: interior design

2020

Hirosaki Contemporary Art Museum
status: competition | 1st prize | ongoing
location: Hirosaki, Japan
date: 2017-
area: 3,537 m²
program: museum

Chiso Building
status: ongoing
location: Kyoto, Japan
date: 2017-
area: 5,500 m²
program: renovation
photo: Frans Parthesius

Yokohama Station Department Store
status: ongoing
location: Yokohama, Japan
date: 2016-
area: 21,370 m²
program: interior design
photo: Frans Parthesius

2021

Bhutan Five Star Village Hotel
status: ongoing
location: Bhutan
date: 2017-
area: 2,800 m²
program: hotel

2022

10 kyoto
status: ongoing
location: Kyoto, Japan
date: 2017-
area: 12,500 m²
program: complex

2027

Scramble Stadium Shibuya
status: ongoing
location: Tokyo, Japan
date: 2018-
area: 30,000 m²
program: stadium

* Projects designed by former practice Dorell.Ghotmeh.
 Tane / Architects.

* Dorell.Ghotmeh.Tane / Architectsの設計によるプロジェクト

Credits

Photos ｜ 写真

Francesco Niki Takehiko pp. 242～245
Frans Parthesius pp. 158～177, pp. 180～198, pp. 200～201, pp. 228～233
Propapanda pp. 114～115
Shinkenchiku-sha pp. 126～127, 130, pp. 132～135, pp. 215～216, pp. 218～219, p. 221, pp. 226～227
Takuji Shimmura pp. 116～121, pp. 124～125, pp. 128～129, p. 131, pp. 136～145, pp. 234～241, pp. 246～247, pp. 250～261
Takumi Ota pp. 202～212
Tõnu Tunnel pp. 122～123
Yuna Yagi pp. 214～215, p. 220, pp. 222～224
Dorell.Ghotmeh.Tane / Architects pp. 146～151
Atelier Tsuyoshi Tane Architects pp. 152～157, pp. 178～179, p. 199, p. 225

*Credits of photos used in the timeline are indicated under the respective photos.
*Timelineについては写真下にクレジットを表記している。

Drawings ｜ 図面

Atelier Tsuyoshi Tane Architects pp. 264～305

Image Credits ｜ 図版

*Images are numbered top left to bottom right on each page.
*図版は掲載ページの左上から右下に向けてナンバーを付している。

Alexandr Khrapichev, University of Oxford,CC BY 4.0 p. 55
Ali and Moon 2007 p. 62-5
Bibliotheca Augustana p. 86-9, 10
Bibliothèque nationale de France pp. 10～11, p. 28-8, p. 32-11, p. 43, p. 44-2, 3, 4, 5, p. 46-1, p. 62-1, p. 92-1, 4, 10, p. 93, p. 102-10, p. 106-3
Charpentier-Richard,CC BY 2.0 p. 46-6
clipartxtras.com p. 32-7
Commission des sciences et arts d'Egypte p. 28-7
Copyright© 2002-2018 - dott. Zoonomo Maurizio Arduin - P.IVA 01405190297 p. 85
Courtesy of Yale University Library p. 86-8
David Bellis p. 62-3
David Gregory & Debbie Marshall,CC BY 4.0 p. 39
Digital Library@Villanova University,CC BY-SA 4.0 p. 28-9
Dr David Furness p. 62-9
Estonian National Museum collections pp. 17～19
Eye Ubiquitous p. 28-10
From The New York Public Library p. 31
Geodatastyrelsen p. 38-2
Heidelberg University Library,CC BY-SA 3.0 p. 56-10
jasminam pp. 12～13
Jidanni,CC BY-SA 3.0 p. 62-4
Kyodo News p. 27
Library of Congress, Geography and Map Division p. 86-12
Map data ©2018 Google p. 44-1, p. 51
Mary Evans Picture Library p. 32-4
MBOU TSO No. 42, Tula city p. 28-1
NASA p. 110-2
Natalia Frei p. 50-9
Reproduction Philippe Berthé / CMN p. 92-8
Richard Powell,CC BY-SA 2.5 p. 110-8
Rob Lavinsky, CC BY-SA-3.0 p. 50-11
Rosenbach Museum & Library p. 106-5
s_minaga p. 32-1
Science Photo Library p. 102-7
Skogshögskolan's archives p. 91
Smithsonian Collection p. 109
©Textualités p. 110-3
The British Library's collections, 2013 p. 67
©The New York Public Library, 2018 p. 46-10
Trevor Saylor p. 56-7
University of Copenhagen p. 38-3
Wellcome Collection, CC BY 4.0 p. 38-4, 5, 6, 7, 8, 9, 10, p. 44-7, p. 45, p. 46-11, p. 50-6, p. 61, p. 62-7, 8, p. 68-3, p. 69, p. 74-7, 8, p. 79, p. 81, p. 86-1, 2, 4, 6, p. 102-1, 2, 3, 4, 5, 6, p. 110-6, 7
一般財団法人雑花園文庫 p. 86-13
大磯町郷土資料館（提供） p. 80-11

大阪府立近つ飛鳥博物館 p. 28-4
学習院大学史料館 p. 98-1
株式会社 千總 p. 73, p. 74-1, 2, 4, 5, 6, p. 75
株式会社 虎屋 p. 97, p. 98-6, 7, 8, 9, 10
京都大学大学院文化研究科考古学研究室 p. 28-5
熊本県教育委員会 p. 28-2
公益財団法人青森県りんご協会 p. 50-2
国営海ノ中道海浜公園事務所（所有） p. 80-5, 6, 7
国立公文書館 p. 25
日本煉瓦製造 p. 50-3
弘前市立弘前図書館 p. 50-5
福嶋家 p. 49, p. 50-4
明治神宮 p. 26
横浜市立図書館 p. 68-2

Dorell.Ghotmeh.Tane / Architects p. 21, p. 23, p. 29, p. 40, p. 44-1, p. 47, p. 58, p. 103, p. 107, p. 111
Atelier Tsuyoshi Tane Architects p. 20, p. 22, p. 32-6, 8, pp. 34～35, p. 41, pp. 51～53, p. 59, pp. 63～65, pp. 70～71, p. 74-3, pp. 76～77, pp. 82～83, pp. 87～89, pp. 94～95, p. 99, p. 101, p. 102-12
public domain pp. 6～7, p. 28-6, p. 32-2, 3, 5, 9, 10, 12, p. 33, p. 37, p. 38-1, p. 44-6, 8, 9, 10, 11, p. 46-2, 3, 4, 5, 7, 8, 9, p. 50-7, 8, 10, pp. 56～57, p. 62-2, 6, p. 68-1, 4, 5, 6, 7, 8, p. 74-9, 10, p. 74-10, 12, p. 74-10, p. 80-3, 10, 11, 12, p. 86-3, 5, 7, 11, p. 92-2, 3, 6, 7, 9, p. 98-2, 3, 4, 5, p. 102-8, 9, 11, p. 105, p. 106-1, 2, 4, 6, 7, 8, 9, 10, 11, 12, p. 110-4, 5

References ｜ 出典

*Images are numbered top left to bottom right on each page.
*図版は掲載ページの左上から右下に向けてナンバーを付している。

p. 25 『文久山陵図』/ 外池昇編 / 新人物往来社 / 2005
p. 26-1, 4, 8, 9 『明治神宮叢書』第14巻（造営編3）/ 明治神宮編 / 明治神宮社務所 / 2003
p. 26-2, 3, 5, 6, 7 『明治神宮叢書』第13巻（造営編2）/ 明治神宮編 / 明治神宮社務所 / 2003
p. 28-2 『熊本県文化財調査報告 オブサン古墳調査編＋修復整備工事編』/ 熊本県教育委員会 / 1987
p. 28-3 『日本古墳大辞典』/ 大塚初重ほか / 東京堂出版編 / 1989
p. 28-4 『考古学からみた日本の古代国家と古代文化：近つ飛鳥博物館展示ガイドブック：もうひとつの飛鳥からみた日本の古代』/ 大阪府立近つ飛鳥博物館 / 2013
p. 28-5 『平成24年度春季特別展王と首長の神まつり−古墳時代の祭祀と信仰−』/ 大阪府立近つ飛鳥博物館図録57 大阪府立近つ飛鳥博物館編 / 2012
p. 28-7 *Description de l'Egypte* / Commission des sciences et arts d'Egypte / C. L. F. Panckoucke, Paris / 1823
p. 28-8 *La galerie agréable du monde* / Van Der Aa, Pieter Boudewyn / Pieter vander AA / 1729
p. 28-9 *Travels of Anacharsis the Younger in Greece* / Barthelemy, J.-J. / J. Johnson, London / 1806
p. 32-10 *Liber de ascensu et decensu intellectus* / Ramon Llull / 1512
p. 32-12 *The ventilation of mines* / Ralph Moore / Maurice Ogle & Son,Glasgow / 1859
p. 43-1, p. 44-3 *Les Illuminations.XIXe s.* / Arthur Rimbaud / 1886
p. 44-2 *Illuminations. Notice par Paul Verlaine* / Arthur Rimbaud / la Vogue, Paris / 1886
p. 44-4, 5 *Poésies complètes* / Arthur Rimbaud / L. Vanier, Paris / 1895
p. 44-6 *POÉSIES* / Arthur Rimbaud / A. Messein, Paris / 1919
p. 44-9 *L'idea del theatro dell'eccellen* / M. Givlio Camillo / Appresso Lorenzo Torrentino,Florence / 1550
p. 44-10 *De umbris idearum* / Giordano Bruno / 1582
p. 44-11 *Thesavrus Artificiosae Memoriae* / Cosimo Rosselli / Antonius Paudanius, Venice / 1579
p. 50-10 *De Bibel overgeset wten Latijn in Duusche : Vol. I.* / Peter Comestor / 1431
p. 56-8 *Avila biblioteca capella* / Johannes Romberch / Melchiorem Sessam / 1533
p. 56-10 *I. B. Piranesi Lapides Capitolini Sive Fasti Consvlares Trivmphalesq* / Piranesi, Giovanni Battista / Piranesi, Rome / 1762
p. 62-6 *Meyers Konversations-Lexikon, 4th ed* / Joseph Meyer / 1885–1892
p. 62-7 *The nursling; the feeding and hygiene of premature and full-term infants* / Pierre Budin / Caxton, London / 1907

p. 62-8 *Des maladies mentales considérées sous les rapports médical, hygiénique et médico-légal* / Etienne Esquirol / J.B. Baillière, Paris / 1838
p. 80-1, 2 「考古学から見た古代日本の住居」『日本古代文化の探求・家』/ 石野博信著 大林太良編 / 社会思想社 / 1975
p. 80-3 『新編鎌倉志』/ 河井恒久 / 大日本地誌大系刊行会 / 1915
p. 80-4 『高根沢町史通年編I』/ 高根沢町編纂委員会 / 高根沢町 / 2000
p. 80-8, 9 『おおいその歴史大磯町史11別編ダイジェスト版』/ 大磯町 / 2009
p. 86-8 *On the growth of plants in closely glazed cases* / Nathaniel Bagshaw Ward / John Van Voorst, Paternoster Row / 1852
p. 86-9, 10 *Taccuinum sanitatis* / Ibn Butlan / 1450
p. 86-11 *POPULAR HISTORY OF THE PALMS* / Berthold Seemann / L. Reeve, London / 1856
p. 92-4 *Le Livre de chasse* / Gaston III / 1301
p. 102-3 *A Journal of Natural Philosophy, Chemistry, and the Arts* / William Nicholson / G. G. and J. Robinson, London / 1797
p. 102-4 *The pulse* / W.H. Broadbent / Cassell, London / 1890
p. 102-10 *REGI,LUDOVICO* / Jan Heweliusz / S. Reiniger, Gedani / 1673
p. 102-11 *Philosophia Moysaica* / Robert Fludd / Petrus Rammazenius, Gouda / 1638
p. 105-1, p. 106-7, 8, 9 *Harmonia Macrocosmica* / Andreas Cellarius / Johannes Janssonius / 1660
p. 106-3 *Principio da verdadeira cosmographia* / Bartholomeu Velho / 1568
p. 106-4 *Petri Apiani Cosmographia per Gemmam* / Petrus Apianus edit by Gemma Frisius / Vaeneunt Antuerpiae / 1539
p. 106-5 *Cosmographia* / Petrus Apianus / apud V. Gaultherot, Paris / 1551
p. 110-4 *Soap bubles, their colours and the forces which mould them* / Boys Charles Vernon / Society for Promoting Christian Knowledge, London / 1916

*Copyright holders of some of the items could not be identified. If you would like to provide related information, please contact our editorial department.
*数点に限り著作権が判明しないものがありました。お心当たりの方は編集部までご連絡ください。

English Translation ｜ 英語翻訳

Kazuko Sakamoto 坂本和子

Proofreading ｜ 校正

Harutaka Oribe 織部晴崇 / English
OURAIDOU K.K. 株式会社鷗来堂 / Japanese

Editorial Collaboration ｜ 編集協力

Atelier Tsuyoshi Tane Architects
Tsuyoshi Tane
Anais Cuillier
Aki Nishida
Dustin Ly
Florencia Yalale
Francisco Javier Roy
Froso Pipi
Isabelle Atkinson-Evans
Lounès Amalou-Yezli
Nanami Endo
Paul Trussler
Ryosuke Yago
Sayaka Kondo
Shota Yamamoto
Takuro Kunitomo
Yosuke Tsukamoto

Acknowledgement

Atelier Tsuyoshi Tane Architects would like to express our sincerest gratitude
to everyone who shared in the vision, passion and conviction that allowed us to
complete this challenge.
We also express our deepest appreciation to the following people and organizations
who's contributions and support have made the realization of this book.

Atelier Tsuyoshi Tane Architects がこれまで活動を続けられたのは、
皆様のご支援とご尽力によるものであり、心より深く感謝の意を表します。

Architectes Français à l'Export
Centre national d'art et de culture Georges Pompidou
Chiso Co., Ltd.
Citizen Watch Co., Ltd.
City of Hirosaki
Columbia University GSAPP
Estonian National Museum
Hase Building Group
Hermès Japon
Hirosaki Art Creation K. K.
Lumine Co., Ltd.
Maison de la Culture du Japon à Paris
City of Paris
Meiji Jingu Research Institute
mina perhonen
Ministry of Culture, Estonia
Nagasaki Prefectural Art Museum
Noism
Piaget S.A.
Renault S.A.S.
Reunion des Musées Nationaux - Grand Palais
RYUTOPIA Niigata City Performing Arts Center
Saito Kinen Festival Matsumoto
Shinkenchiku-sha Co., Ltd.
Shiseido Co., Ltd.
Spiral
Taka Ishii Gallery
Tokyo Metropolitan Art Museum
Tokyo Metropolitan Government
Tokyo Opera City Art Gallery
Toraya France S.A.R.L
Toshiba Corporation
Yamaguchi Center for Arts and Media
21_21 Design Sight

Special Thanks
Dan Dorell
Lina Ghotmeh

Akemi Sano
Akira Minagawa
Bas Smets
Fumio Nanjo
Hanno Grossschmidt
Herve Audibert
Izumi Okayasu
Jo Kanamori
Junko Ichihara
Kari Bachmann
Kazuhiro Shioike
Kishin Shinoyama
Klaas de Rycke
Krista Aru
Kumiko Ikada
Laurent Beccaria
Masato Okada
Michel Forgue
Naoko Seki
Peeter Mauer
Pille Lausmae
Sayaka Kase
Setsuko Klossowska de Rola
Shino Nomura
Sophie de Sivry
Tadashi Sano
Taichi Saito
Takayuki Ishii
Tiit Sild
Tomomi Hayashi
Yahoko Sasao
Yasuhiro Kaneda
Yoshiko Imaizumi
Yutaka Endo

Profile

Tsuyoshi Tane

1979   Born in Tokyo, Japan
2002   Graduated from Hokkaido Tokai University in Japan
2003   Post-graduate program at The Royal Danish Academy of fine Arts in Denmark
2003-04   Worked at Henning Larsen Architects in Denmark
2004-05   Worked at David Adjaye Associates in UK
2006-16   Co-founder Architect Dorell.Ghotmeh.Tane / Architects in France
2012-   Adjunct professor at Columbia University, GSAPP NY/PARIS in France
2014-   Visiting professor at ESVMD in Switzerland
2017   Founder architect Atelier Tsuyoshi Tane Architects in France

AWARDS

2006   1st Prize Winner | Estonian National Museum | Estonia
2008   Award Nouveaux Albums des Jeunes Architectes 07-08 | French Ministry of Culture | France
　　　　Rassegna Lombarda di architettura under 40 Award | Italy
2010   Nomination for The Ian Chernikhov Prize 2010 | Architecture Prize for architects under 40 | Russia
　　　　10 for 2010 Visionary Architects for a New Decade | Euroepean Architect Review | UK
2012   Finalist of The New National Stadium of Japan | Kofun Stadium | Japan
2013   Award Red Dot Award Winner | The Bump | Germany
　　　　iF Design Award | Frozen Time | Germany
2014   Milan Design Award 2014 Best Entertaining + Best Sound | LIGHT is TIME | Italy
　　　　1st Prize Winner | Bolzano IPES Building | Italy
2016   Academie d'architecture Prix Dejean award | France
　　　　AFEX Grand Prix 2016 | Estonian National Museum | France
　　　　AFEX Prix 2016 | A House for Oiso | France
　　　　CCI Paris IDF Award | Toraya Paris | France
　　　　1st Prize Winner | Réinventer Paris | Réalimenter Masséna | France
2017   Estonian Cultural Endowment Grand Prix | Estonian National Museum | Estonia
　　　　Estonian Association of Architects Annual Award 2017 | Estonian National Museum | Estonia
　　　　The 67th Ministry of Education and Fine Art New-Face Awards | Japan
　　　　Nomination for Mies van der Rohe EU Award | Estonian National Museum | EU
　　　　1st Prize Winner | Hirosaki Contemporary Art Museum | Japan
　　　　Best Public Building Award | Estonian National Museum | Estonia
　　　　Best Concrete Building of the Year | Estonian National Museum | Estonia
　　　　Archmarathon 2017 Art & Culture Winner | Estonian National Museum | Italy
2018   European Museum Forum Awards 2018 | Estonian National Museum | EU

田根 剛

1979   東京都生まれ
2002   北海道東海大学芸術工学部建築学科卒業
2003   デンマーク王立芸術学院・客員研究員
2003-04   ヘニング・ラーセン・アーキテクツ勤務 | コペンハーゲン・デンマーク
2004-05   アジャイ・アソシエイツ勤務 | ロンドン・イギリス
2006-16   Dorell.Ghotmeh.Tane / Architects 設立 | パリ・フランス
2012-   コロンビア大学 GSAPP NY/PARIS 講師 | パリ・フランス
2014-   ESVND 大学院 客員教授 | スイス
2017   Atelier Tsuyoshi Tane Architects 設立 | パリ・フランス

主な受賞歴

2006   エストニア国立博物館国際設計競技・最優秀賞 | エストニア国立博物館 | エストニア
2008   フランス文化庁新進建築家賞 07-08 | フランス
　　　　ミラノ建築家協会賞 | イタリア
2010   イアン・チェルニコフ賞・ノミネート | ロシア
　　　　10 for 2010 Visionary Architects 次世代賞 | ヨーロッパ・アーキテクト・レビュー | イギリス
2012   新国立競技場基本構想国際デザイン競技・最終選考 | 古墳スタジアム | 日本
2013   Red dot Award Winner 賞 | The Bump | ドイツ
　　　　iF デザイン・アワード | Frozen Time | ドイツ
2014   ミラノ・デザイン・アワード 2014 Best Entertaining + Best Sound | LIGHT is TIME | イタリア
　　　　ボルツァーノ住宅局社屋設計競技・最優秀賞 | イタリア
2016   フランス建築アカデミー新人賞 | フランス
　　　　フランス国外建築賞グランプリ | エストニア国立博物館 | フランス
　　　　フランス国外建築賞 | A House for Oiso | フランス
　　　　CCI Paris IDF 賞 | Toraya Paris | フランス
　　　　Réinventer Paris マセナ駅跡地計画・最優秀賞 | Réalimenter Masséna | フランス
2017   エストニア文化大賞 | エストニア国立博物館 | エストニア
　　　　エストニア建築家協会賞 | エストニア国立博物館 | エストニア
　　　　第 67 回芸術選奨文部科学大臣新人賞 | 日本
　　　　ミース・ファンデル・ローエ賞ノミネート | エストニア国立博物館 | EU
　　　　仮称）弘前市芸術文化施設設計競技・最優秀賞 | 日本
　　　　エストニア・ベスト・パブリック・ビルディング賞 | エストニア国立博物館 | エストニア
　　　　ベスト・コンクリート・ビルディング賞 | エストニア国立博物館 | エストニア
　　　　アーキマラソン・アート＆文化部門最優秀賞 | エストニア国立博物館 | イタリア
2018   ヨーロッパ美術館フォーラム・アワード 2018 | エストニア国立博物館 | EU

Atelier Tsuyoshi Tane Architects

Founder Architect
Tsuyoshi Tane

Project Architects
Haruki Nakayama
Iwona Szczepanska
Kuniyuki Okuyama
Matthew Nowicki
Paul Trussler
Valentino Pagani

Architects
Aoi Akimoto
Fernando Cremades
Francisco Javier Roy
Froso Pipi
Isabelle Atkinson-Evans
Kenji Hada
Mathilde Despinois
Matteo Lunanova
Misaki Nozawa
Romain Alies
Ryosuke Yago
Shota Yamamoto

Designer
Yosuke Tsukamoto

Graphic Designer
Anais Cuillier

Administration & Communication
Elsa Willmott
Sayaka Kondo

Former Staff Members
Emanuele Piersanti
Lou Fery
Naoki Hayasaka
Paul Rabasse

TSUYOSHI TANE　Archaeology of the Future
田根 剛建築作品集　未来の記憶

2018年10月24日　初版第1刷発行
2025年 2月17日　初版第5刷発行

著者：田根 剛

発行者：渡井 朗
発行所：TOTO出版（TOTO株式会社）
〒107-0062 東京都港区南青山1-24-3 TOTO乃木坂ビル2F
[営業] TEL：03-3402-7138　FAX：03-3402-7187
[編集] TEL：03-3497-1010
URL：https://jp.toto.com/publishing

デザイン：林 琢真
印刷・製本：株式会社サンニチ印刷

落丁本・乱丁本はお取り替えいたします。
本書の全部又は一部に対するコピー・スキャン・デジタル化等の無断複製行為は、
著作権法上での例外を除き禁じます。本書を代行業者等の第三者に依頼してスキャン
やデジタル化することは、たとえ個人や家庭内での利用であっても著作権法上認めら
れておりません。
定価はカバーに表示してあります。

© 2018 Tsuyoshi Tane

Printed in Japan
ISBN978-4-88706-376-1